PALETAS

PALETAS

AUTHENTIC RECIPES FOR

mexican ice pops, shaved ice & aguas frescas

Fany Gerson

Photography by Ed Anderson
& Paul O'Hanlon

TEN SPEED PRESS
Berkeley

CONTENTS

Acknowledgments **vii**

Introduction **1**

paletas
ice pops 19

PALETAS DE FRESA
Strawberry Ice Pops **21**

PALETAS DE ZARZAMORA
Blackberry Ice Pops **22**

PALETAS DE MELÓN
Cantaloupe Ice Pops **23**

PALETAS DE SANDÍA
Watermelon Ice Pops **24**

PALETAS DE TORONJA
Grapefruit Ice Pops **25**

PALETAS DE AGUACATE
Avocado Ice Pops **26**

PALETAS DE LIMÓN
Lime Ice Pops **28**

PALETAS DE CHABACANO Y MANZANILLA
Apricot-Chamomile Ice Pops **29**

PALETAS DE JAMAICA CON FRAMBUESA
Hibiscus-Raspberry Ice Pops **31**

PALETAS DE PIÑA CON CHILE
Spicy Pineapple Ice Pops **32**

PALETAS DE DONAJÍ
Mezcal-Orange Ice Pops **35**

PALETAS DE SANGRITA
Spiced Tomato-Tequila
Ice Pops **36**

PALETAS DE CREMA Y CEREZA
CON TEQUILA
Sour Cream, Cherry,
and Tequila Ice Pops **37**

PALETAS DE YOGURT CON MORAS
Yogurt Ice Pops with Berries **40**

PALETAS DE PLÁTANO ROSTIZADO
Roasted Banana Ice Pops **43**

PALETAS DE MARACUYÁ
Passion Fruit Cream Pops **45**

PALETAS DE PAY DE LIMÓN
Lime Pie Ice Pops **48**

PALETAS DE COCO RÁPIDAS
Quick Coconut Ice Pops **50**

PALETAS DE COCO FRESCO
Fresh Coconut Ice Pops **53**

PALETAS DE NUEZ
Pecan Ice Pops **55**

PALETAS DE CHOCOLATE
Mexican Chocolate Ice Pops **57**

PALETAS DE ROMPOPE
Mexican Eggnog Ice Pops **59**

PALETAS DE CAJETA
Caramel Ice Pops **60**

PALETAS DE ARROZ CON LECHE
Rice Pudding Ice Pops **62**

raspados
shaved ices 65

RASPADO DE MORAS
Berry Shaved Ice 67

RASPADO ROJO
Red Shaved Ice 68

RASPADO DE TAMARINDO
Tamarind Shaved Ice 70

RASPADO DE OREJONES
Dried Apricot Shaved Ice 72

RASPADO DE PIÑA COLADA
Piña Colada Shaved Ice 73

RASPADO DE HORCHATA CON FRESAS
Strawberry-Horchata Shaved
Ice 74

RASPADO DE ROMPOPE
Mexican Eggnog Shaved Ice 77

GLORIAS
Veracruz-Style Shaved Ice 79

MANGONADAS
Spicy Mango Ice 80

GRANIZADO DE MICHELADA
Beer with Chile Granita 83

GRANIZADO DE QUESO CON
MANZANAS Y PILONCILLO
Queso Fresco Granita
with Syrupy Apples 84

aguas frescas
refreshing drinks 87

AGUA DE PEPINO CON LIMÓN
Cucumber-Lime Cooler 89

AGUA DE LIMÓN CON CHÍA
Limeade with Chia Seeds 91

NARANJADA
Fizzy Orange Cooler 92

CONGA
Mixed Fruit Punch 94

AGUA DE PIÑA CON ALFALFA Y LIMÓN
Pineapple-Alfalfa-Lime Cooler 95

AGUA DE GUAYABA
Guava Cooler 96

AGUA DE JAMAICA
Hibiscus Cooler 97

LÁGRIMAS DE LA VIRGEN
Beet Cooler with Fruits 101

HORCHATA DE PEPITA DE MELÓN
Cantaloupe Seed Horchata 103

POLVILLO
Cacao-Corn Drink 105

HORCHATA DE ARROZ
Cinnamon-Rice Drink 107

AGUA DE TAMARINDO
Tamarind Cooler 109

Index 111

Measurement Conversion
Charts 116

ACKNOWLEDGMENTS

Sometimes I think I wrote this book in my dreams since I started it during the same very busy summer when I launched my paleta company, La Newyorkina. Many people helped me during that time, making paletas, selling them, or supporting me in countless other ways.

First I have to thank Melissa Moore, my friend and editor, for having the vision for this book and sharing my enthusiasm for the frozen treats of Mexico. As with my first book, designer Katy Brown made everything so beautiful and captured the flavor of Mexico with her incredible aesthetic sense and wonderful artistic eye. I feel blessed because everyone at Ten Speed has been wonderful to work with and I look forward to a continuous, fruitful relationship for years to come.

Speaking of lasting relationships, I would've never had the opportunity to write these books without my agent, Lisa Queen, whom I admire and care about deeply.

Including aguas frescas recipes in this cookbook would seem obvious because they go hand in hand with paleta making, but I have to thank my dear friend Alex for the idea. She is a continuous source of inspiration and support, for which I am deepy grateful.

It's hard to express my enormous gratitude to Eric, who has been there for me from the very beginning. Without him, we might not have had any paletas for La Newyorkina's opening weekend. More importantly, I will forever be grateful for his continuous kindness, support, and love.

I owe many thanks to my grandmother Ana because her words of wisdom have given me strength in the toughest moments; I don't think she realizes how much she has inspired me to follow my dreams. And she went out of her way to get me the molds and bags I needed to make the paletas! She is simply a beautiful and awesome person.

For countless reasons, my dad is the person in my life I admire most. His thirst for knowledge and incredible inner strength continuously inspire me to push myself in every aspect of life. I am incredibly grateful for all he has done for me.

My mother introduced me to the wonderful sweetness of Mexico—even though she doesn't like to admit that she has a quite a sweet tooth. My earliest memories of eating paletas are with her. She has always shown me to appreciate and value food through the quality of ingredients, and to take pride in what we do.

Life is simply more fun because of my siblings, nicknamed Yaelita and Jaisi Fus. Their love has carried me through the best and worst of times, and I am very, very fortunate to have them in my life and for the incredible bond that exists between us.

Manolo has been a hard critic since I was a little girl, but he does it to motivate me to push myself further and not be a conformist, and because he cares deeply. I love that about him! He is one of the most passionate people I know and that certainly rubs off and inspires those around him. I treasure his love and support tremendously.

Enormous gratitude goes to my friend Hannah, with whom I was fortunate to share the birth of La Newyorkina. I learned a lot from her and look forward to many more years of friendship. Despite a broken nose, broken down freezers, melty paletas, sweaty days, heavy pushcarts, and long hours, I'll forever treasure that crazy and fun startup summer—I don't think I could've done it without her.

I am very grateful to all the people and friends who have supported me since the beginning of the paleta whirlwind. Thank you to my friends whom I call my NY family—you know who you are! Special thanks to one of my oldest friends here, Ian, since he's responsible for the name La Newyorkina. I am grateful that we can bounce around creative ideas, and for his continuous encouragement and belief in me.

To Chulis, Silvis, and Adis, three amazing friends who have been there for me in countless ways, you get a thank you with a big hug attached. To Joab and Yosi, much gratitude for lending us the apartment for the photo shoot (and to Yosi for being in one of the photographs), and for sharing my enthusiasm for delicious paletas.

I can't forget my dear friend Sandy, whom I don't see nearly enough as I'd like to but always feel her close. Her daughter, Alex, was an incredibly natural paleta model and can't thank Sandy enough for letting us include her in the book.

Photographs are so important whenever food is involved because they transport and entice you, capturing what words can't convey. While working on this book I learned that paletas are not the easiest subjects to photograph, so I have enormous admiration and gratitude for Paul and Ed's talent. I admire them professionally and am also very grateful for the friendships that have developed.

I need to thank all the people I met at the markets, both passionate producers of delicious treats, like Kareem and Julian, and all the customers with whom I was able to share a refreshing and delicious part of my culture.

Lastly, I'd like to recognize the hard work of famers, paleteros, and street vendors in Mexico. They are responsible for many of the sweet traditions and deliciousness of my country. Their work ethic, passion, pride, and attitude are examples to me and am enormously grateful to them.

INTRODUCTION

The first frozen treats in Mexico were made with snow collected at the top of the Popocatépetl and Iztaccíhuatl volcanoes. At first, the snow was carried down and used to refrigerate things like medicine and food, but later people realized they could pair the snow with sweet fruits to make luxurious frozen treats.

The enjoyment of frozen treats is something almost universal. They're beloved all over the world, especially by children. The fact that they're so widespread is quite remarkable when you consider the great variety in the different cultures and cuisines where they appear. Italians have their granitas and gelatos, Argentineans their *helados*, Indians their *kulfi*, and Japanese their *mochi*. And, yes, Mexicans have their paletas, which are savored throughout the country, all year round. Although paletas are the main focus of this book, I've also included recipes for two other types of refreshing Mexican treats: raspados, which are similar to granitas, and the beverages known as aguas frescas.

paletas

Paleterías (paleta shops), with their bright awnings and storefronts, are part of the Mexican landscape, decorating the streets with their vivid colors. And like many other fortunate children in my home country, I grew up enjoying paletas on a regular basis.

Although paletas have become popular outside of Mexico, you may not be familiar with them, so let me tell you a bit about them. The word *paleta* derives from *palo*, meaning "stick," a reference to how they're made and eaten. They're essentially ice pops: delicious flavored liquids, frozen with a stick to hold as you eat them. Paletas come in countless flavors and are made from an enormous variety of fruits, nuts, and other ingredients, including spices and even flowers. They're most commonly made in a rectangle shape. Paletas may have a smooth consistency, but they often include chunks of some sort to provide texture and trap different flavors.

In Mexico, we have two different types of paletas. The most popular type is *paletas de agua*, which are typically made with fresh fruit, water, sweetener (usually sugar from sugarcane), and sometimes other flavorings. Popular flavors include lime, watermelon, tamarind, mango, chile, and coconut.

The second type is *paletas de leche* or *paletas de crema*, which are made with some kind of dairy (usually whole milk or heavy cream) and flavorings or fruit. Sadly, these days most commercial *paletas de leche* are made with a powdered base due to the price of milk, but those that are still made with fresh milk or cream are incredibly delicious. They're like ice cream on a stick, often studded with delicious fresh fruit, but also combined with other ingredients, such as pecans, chocolate, *cajeta* (goat's milk caramel), *rompope* (similar to eggnog), and rice.

Although there are many flavors of paletas, the most common varieties have one main flavor. That's probably because the majority are made with fresh fruit, which is great on its own. When other flavors and ingredients are added to fruit paletas, they're usually there only to enhance the natural succulence of the fruit.

There are a few things that make paletas noteworthy. The first is that they are found everywhere in Mexico. They're

often sold from carts, but it's
more common to find them in
paleterías. In fact, I have yet
to encounter a Mexican town,
no matter how small, without
a *paletería*. These shops typically have a clear freezer you
can look down into and see an
amazing rainbow of perfectly
lined-up paletas. I remember being really, really, *really*
excited when I was big enough
to stand on my tippy toes and
peek in (although being picked
up gave me a better view).

The second thing that's
exceptional about paletas is the
incredible array of flavors. This
is mostly because of the wide
variety of fruit that abounds in Mexico, which is also one of
the most exciting things about the food in Mexico. From more
familiar fruits like strawberries, apricots, blackberries, melons, tangerines, and other citrus fruits to the tropical flavors
of mango, guava, passion fruit, and coconut, to the exotic, like
tamarind, mamey, prickly pear, and soursop, the list goes on
and on. Even some of the fruits we usually think of as veg-
etables, like avocados, tomatoes, and chile peppers, make
an appearance in paletas, as well as flowers like roses and
hibiscus.

Another thing that makes paletas special is how the flavors have been adapted to the modern palate and embrace the
sweet, salty, spicy, and sour flavors Mexicans love. There are
paletas studded with chunks of fruit and chile peppers, others
made with *chamoy* (a pickled plum or apricot sauce), and some

are even so completely covered with ground piquín chiles that you can't even see the color of the paleta.

Lastly, I think it is truly remarkable that most *paleterías* are family businesses, and that these frozen treats are usually made in an artisanal way. Many families buy their produce from markets then peel, chop, and puree the fresh goods by hand. In these family-run businesses, each person has his or her task—after all, they're helping provide for one another.

There's some debate about the birthplace of paletas, but the most common belief is that they originated in the town of Tocumbo, which is in the state of Michoacán. If you can imagine it, as you enter the town you're welcomed by a humongous pink concrete statue in the shape of a paleta with what looks like a bite taken out of it, and in the space where that bite was taken is a globe that looks like a scoop of ice cream. The statue is a source of great pride for the townspeople.

Sugarcane grows well in the area surrounding Tocumbo, and for years it was a mainstay of the local economy. But growing sugarcane means a lot of hard labor for very little return, so in the early 1900s, Tocumbo remained a tiny village where it was difficult to make a living. In 1930, Rafael Malfavón opened a small *paletería*, distributing his frozen treats to the townspeople and neighboring villagers using donkeys that carried wooden boxes that Señor Malfavón had designed especially for this purpose.

Though Rafael Malfavón may have been first, the expansion that followed has been attributed to others. Legend has it that in the mid-1940s, three men who had been selling paletas in Tocumbo for a few years—brothers Ignacio and Luis Alcázar and their friend Agustín Andrade—headed to Mexico City to open the first *paletería* there. They called their shop La Michoacana, and although they were illiterate, they achieved success beyond their wildest dreams. They ended up selling franchises to everyone they knew—friends, cousins, neighbors, acquaintances. Since then, La Michoacana has become one of the largest franchises in Mexico, with more than fifteen thousand outlets, and more than a thousand in Mexico City alone! So now you know why it's said that all the best *paleteros* (paleta makers) are from Tocumbo, no matter where you are in Mexico.

In a way, all of these people from Tocumbo are related to one another, and even if they spend most of the year elsewhere selling paletas, most keep a home in Tocumbo to return to for the holidays. And it should come as no surprise that Tocumbo holds a weeklong *feria de paletas* (paletas fair) at the end of the year. You try many new and different flavors of paletas at the fair, but it's really more a celebration of the town and its people, who have not only kept their tradition alive, but also expanded to the point where the most common names for *paleterías* are La Michoacana, Tocumbo, and La Flor de Michoacan, including in the United States.

While this story seems well established, another legend has it that paletas originated in the town of Mexticacán, in the neighboring state of Jalisco. In the early 1940s, a man by the name of Genarito Jáuregui, apparently a jack-of-all-trades, somehow got hold of a German machine that compacted ice. As the story goes, his compadre Don Celso de Cañadas de Obregón told him about a *paletera* (paleta machine) that was abandoned in the customs office in the state of Veracruz. It is said that Señor Jáuregui partnered up with another compadre, Tilde Rios, to buy the machine.

Back then, Jáuregui was managing a corn mill and several fields, so it fell to Rios to run the *paletería*. The *paletera* could only make one hundred paletas at a time, and they used donkeys to haul water to the *paletería*. Their business was successful enough that soon they bought a more modern machine. After a few years, many other people from Mexticacán jumped on the bandwagon, opening *paleterías* throughout Mexico.

In Mexico, most towns have a plaza or main square with some sort of monument or statue of a famous historical person. In Mexticacán, this monument is dedicated to the paleta, which is the town's main source of income. The monument is a pyramid with a plaque with a carved paleta on one side. And just like in Tocumbo, Mexticacán has a festival dedicated to the paleta: the Heladexpo, one of the biggest fairs in the trade.

So you see, paletas have a long history in Mexico, and a significant place in Mexican cuisine. As far back as I can remember, paletas were part of my life growing up in Mexico. Back home, we're blessed with an incredible cornucopia of fruits, and all of them make their way into paletas. When I came to the United States, I was so surprised, and so sad, to discover that the familiar colorful frozen treats filled with chunks of fruit and bright, fresh flavors were not so easily found. Most markets offered only artificially flavored pops in limited flavors. Tamarind, soursop, and prickly pear ice pops were nowhere to be found!

After living with this for many years, I decided to change the situation by starting my own *paletería*, but I was struggling to come up with a name. One day I was in a cab with two dear friends, Ian and Buho. We were talking about how long we'd been living in New York, and I ventured that I was a real New Yorker because I'd been living in the city for ten years. The conversation moved to other topics, and at some point I asked them to help me come up with a name for my enterprise. Ian turned around and said, "Why don't you follow the idea of La Michoacana and call it La Newyorkina?" Buho and I looked at each other and smiled—we both knew it was right. So La Newyorkina (meaning "the girl from New York") was born.

I began making and selling my paletas at the Hester Street Fair in downtown New York on weekends, changing flavors often depending on what was in season and what I was craving. They were received with great enthusiasm. I'm glad that

La Newyorkina has given me the opportunity to share these delicious treats with New Yorkers—and that I could share a few recipes with even more people in my previous cookbook, *My Sweet Mexico*.

When I decided to start making my own paletas and selling them, one of the first things I did was find some smaller molds so I could make mini paletas. When I was little, there was a special *paletería* that my mom knew about that made miniature paletas, and I was wild about them. I was always the first one to volunteer anytime we had to bring something for school, and the paletería was kind enough to pack the paletas for my classmates in a cooler with ice. I couldn't get enough!

While testing the recipes for *My Sweet Mexico*, I found that the chapter on frozen treats was one of the most fun—and the one with the most volunteers eager to sample the results. As I tested the recipes, I filled my freezer with colorful paletas and

sorbets again and again, and they quickly disappeared every time as friends asked for more. I'm certain your experience will be the same.

Just promise me a few things: use fresh ingredients, get creative, and, most importantly, have fun!

PALETAS BASICS

Ingredients It is no surprise that the quality of your ingredients can make all the difference in the end result of these recipes. When buying fruit to make paletas, choose fruit that is in season, if possible, and the ripest you can get. You can often get discounts on blemished fruit at farmers' markets; this fruit may be too mushy to sell, but it's perfect for paletas since the flavor and natural sugars will be at their best. Some ingredients, like guavas, may be hard to find fresh—in those cases, I recommend using high-quality frozen purees.

Many of these recipes are sweetened with natural cane sugar because that's how most paletas are made in Mexico. Feel free to experiment and adjust the sweetness to fit your tastes, but keep in mind two basic things: in general, frozen foods taste less sweet than they do at room temperature, and the pops won't freeze if they have too much sugar.

You'll also see that a few recipes use alcohol. It's fine to add more if you'd like, just remember that, although alcohol enhances flavor, it doesn't freeze; so if you add too much, you'll end up with drinks instead of paletas.

Some paletas are made with natural stabilizers like gelatin, agar agar, guar gum, and xantham gum, but I left these out. I don't have anything against them—they are quite beneficial for creating paletas that are uniform and sold commercially, but making sure all of my paletas are identical isn't a priority. For the most part, the difference is unnoticeable.

Molds There are many molds out there. Most are made from plastic or silicone and come in all shapes and sizes, from the standard rectangle shape to little umbrella-like ones and even rocket ships. You can also make your own molds by using disposable cups, shot glasses, or any vessel that isn't too wide (to avoid heavy paletas) and has smooth sides. Be creative! Keep in mind that the yields will vary depending on the size of the molds you use. (I tested the recipes for this book in standard 2.5 ounce plastic molds.) With these molds, you'll need to insert the sticks after the paletas have been in the freezer for some time and have a slushy consistency.

Some conventional molds have tight-fitting lids that allow you to insert the sticks from the beginning so you don't have to wait till they're semi-frozen. Although this may sound convenient, it is sometimes a pain to remove the lids, so I prefer to forego them. Lastly, there are modern instant pop makers that must be prefrozen, as you would an ice cream maker. They are more expensive, but allow you to make paletas much more rapidly—some freeze the pops in as little as ten minutes. They only fit a few pops at a time, but you can freeze batches back-to-back as long as the base remains frozen.

Molding No matter which mold you choose, remember that the paleta mixture will expand once it freezes—so when filling the mold, leave at least a ¼-inch space from the top to allow for expansion. If your paleta mixture has a particularly liquidy consistency, it'll expand even more. Use a container with a pouring spout to make it easier to fill the molds.

If your paletas have chunks of fruit or other goodies, you have a couple of options for filling the molds. You'll see that most recipes instruct you to pour a portion of base liquid into the molds and partially freeze (usually for about 50 minutes), then distribute the chunks among the molds, top with the rest of the base, and freeze thoroughly. This is so the chunks won't sink to the bottom of the mold and end up concentrated at the top of the paleta. However, if you're not a stickler for even distribution, feel free to skip this step and add the chunks at the same time as the base and freeze it all in once step.

You can also mix and match flavors you like using this partial freezing technique. Create layers of colors and textures by pouring a bit of one flavor into the mold and partially freezing it, then putting another on top; continue in the same manner, layering as desired.

Freezing To get the best results, adjust the temperature of your freezer so it's at the coldest setting and avoid opening and closing the door. The top shelf is usually the coldest, so try to fit your molds there. Make sure you allow enough space around them so air can circulate better and, therefore, freeze your paletas faster.

The longer the paletas stay in the mold, the better formed they will be. However, don't leave them for more than two weeks, as they might begin to crystallize.

Unmolding To unmold paletas from most types of molds, all you need to do is to dip them in a bit of warm water. I find that if you use a deep container that allows you to submerge the whole mold (I often use the sink), then you can unmold them quite easily. Once you have unmolded them, put each paleta in a resealable bag and store them in the freezer (for up to 6 weeks). There are a couple of sources for specially tailored plastic wrappers like the ones in the avocado paletas photos (page 27), but they usually require a large quantity purchase, so resealable plastic bags are a good alternative. Or, if you happen to go to Mexico, you can find them at many central markets in the big cities.

raspados

The second chapter in this book is devoted to other frozen treats, especially raspados—shaved ice confections somewhat like snow cones. Raspados are delicious, refreshing desserts that melt into slushy beverages, making them the perfect accompaniment to a hot, sunny day—and explaining why they're often served with both a spoon and a straw. Of all the frozen treats, these are definitely the sweetest, but the ice cuts the sweetness quite a bit.

The word *raspado* comes from *raspar*, which means "to scrape," which is the traditional way of making small bits of ice that will soak up the flavor from the syrup that's poured over them. Most *raspados* in Mexico are made by scraping or shaving a big block of ice with a metal hand scraper or shaver, which is done individually for each serving. The ice is usually placed in a cup, banged down, pressed, and transferred to a slightly larger cup and drizzled with syrup. Other times, the ice is delicately placed in a cup and banged lightly so it packs down just a bit and you can fit more ice. In the end, the ice is mounded up to look like the top of a volcano.

These days, some shops use modern machines to do the work. This creates larger chunks of ice that have more texture but don't absorb the syrup as well. You can use a shaved ice machine for the recipes in this book, but unless you use it frequently, it will probably be one of those things that ends up in some corner of your closet for years to come. It might be fun to order a large piece of ice to shave by hand for a large party, but for practical purposes, I think a good blender crushes the ice just fine.

Most of the syrups used on raspados are made with fruit and a water base, but some fruits lend themselves well to a dairy base. Syrups can also be made with preserved fruits, like canned mangoes or peaches in syrup. These days, the syrups used commercially are often cloyingly sweet and made with artificial ingredients. Fortunately, some vendors still use syrups made with natural fruits and sugar. These are still pretty sweet, but they're so good!

In the warmer states of Mexico and on the coasts, you'll find small pushcarts offering raspados, with a tantalizing array of syrups in slender glass bottles—flavors like coconut, peach, rose petals, tamarind, and mango, and, of course, some spicy ones. Some also include delicious chunks of fruit (and plenty of them!), condensed milk, *rompope, cajeta, chamoy,* cinnamon, cocoa powder, toasted coconut, nuts . . . you get the picture. These little carts pack a lot of flavor, and many of the vendors have special creations of their own.

One of the best ones, in my opinion, is offered in Concordia, in the state of Sinaloa. It's made with plums, which grow abundantly in the region, and *leche quemada,* which literally means "burnt milk" but is actually a delicious caramel-like confection. If you ever go to Concordia, you absolutely must try it. I tried to re-create it, but you need to make the caramel with raw milk to get the best results, so I haven't included a recipe for it here. In Colima, they make a version with *leche quemada* that's prepared by making a caramel and cooking it until it's quite dark, then adding milk.

I've also included a couple of granitas, which are a different approach to a similar dessert. With granitas, a flavored liquid is frozen, with ice crystals being scraped off periodically, so that

you end up with an ice infused with flavor, rather than flavored with a syrup as with raspados. You can also use leftover aguas frescas to make granitas by putting the liquid in a shallow pan, letting it set in the freezer, then raking it with a fork.

A funny thing happened when I went to Veracruz to do research for *My Sweet Mexico*. My dear friend Silvia, whom I was staying with at the time, was taking me around the state to show me all the wonderful sweets they had. At one point, she asked me if I had tried *glorias*. Thinking she was talking about a kind of pecan caramel from northern Mexico, I quickly replied yes and told her I loved them. She looked at me strangely and said, "Really, don't you find them super sweet?" (In Spanish, we actually have a word for something that is so sweet that you feel the cavities forming as you eat it: *empalagoso*.) I responded, "They are a bit sweet, but they're small. They're one of my favorites, and I can have one right after another." When it dawned on us that we were talking about two different things, we burst out laughing.

It turns out that in Veracruz, *glorias* are a traditional raspado combination made with bananas or strawberries, vanilla, cinnamon, grosellas syrup, and condensed milk (page 79). I'd never had it before, so off we went to sample some. And yes, it was *empalagoso* at first, but once the ice melted, it was practically perfect, though still a little too much for me. A friend of Silvia's who was with us gladly finished off mine, even though he had already had one of his own.

And by the way, *glorias* means "glorious," and that's the perfect word to describe the feeling of eating a raspado on a hot, sunny day.

aguas frescas

Aguas frescas (literally, "fresh water") are refreshing coolers or drinks that fall somewhere between sodas and juices. They're made from fruit, seeds, grains, nuts, herbs, or a combination of ingredients and are usually sweetened with sugar (from sugarcane). An agua fresca is the perfect way to quench your thirst while strolling around on a warm day, and also perfect for balancing out spicy and full-flavored Mexican cuisine.

When I think of aguas frescas, I immediately get transported to my childhood—to our family kitchen, to be precise. *Agua de tamarindo* (tamarind cooler) has always been my favorite. My sister and I often helped peel the tamarind pods in the kitchen while watching *novelas* (television shows similar to soap operas). My mom didn't let us watch much TV, so it was a kind of guilty pleasure. I inevitably got a stomachache from eating way too much tamarind while we were doing the peeling. Still, I couldn't wait to get home from school the next day because I knew *agua de tamarindo* would be there waiting for me. Yael, my awesome sister, also liked *agua de tamarindo*, but she really preferred *agua de jamaica* (hibiscus cooler) and inevitably marveled at the beautiful magenta color of the water infused with hibiscus flowers.

Aguas frescas have been around since pre-Hispanic times. When Aztecs traveled from their farmlands to the markets in Tenochtitlán (what is now Mexico City), they would paddle through channels in the valley's wetlands and mash some ripe fruit with water as a way to refresh themselves through the journey. Fresh fruit has always been abundant and available, and indigenous people would mash the sweet, overripe fruit then mix it with water to make a refreshing drink. In fact, it is said that when Aztecs from outer territories traveled to Tenochtitlán, they would have aguas frescas to cool off during their journey.

Aguas frescas are sometimes made with certain plants and seeds that have medicinal properties. For example, *agua de nopal*, made with cactus pads, is good for the kidneys; *agua de papaya* helps circulation; *agua de coco* is said to increase sperm count; and *agua de mango* is used for eye disorders and throat infections.

Walking through markets and plazas in Mexico, you'll see lovely large barrel-like glass jars, called *vitroleros*, filled with ice and colorful aguas frescas. The refreshing beverages within are often made from fruits such as pineapple, watermelon, guava, lime, and papaya, but they may also be made with nuts, seeds, and other ingredients. For example, *horchata de pepita de melón* is made from the seeds of the cantaloupe, and *horchata de almendra* is made from rice, cinnamon, and almonds. Before ladling a serving into your cup, the vendor stirs the agua to mix in the pulp that has settled to the bottom. You'll hear the ice clinking against the glass, sort of like a prelude for what you're about to taste. Mmm, I get so excited and thirsty just thinking about it! You'll also find *vitroleros* full of aguas frescas in restaurants and *paleterías* and at street stands.

In Mexico, lunch is the biggest and most important meal of the day and is typically served around three in the afternoon. Parents often go home from work for an hour to enjoy this meal with their family, and although the food served varies widely, it is usually accompanied by a large pitcher of agua fresca. Like many families in Mexico, my family always ate lots of fruit when I was growing up, and our aguas were often made with leftover fruit from breakfast or overripe fruit that we needed to use up.

As with much of the cuisine of Mexico, there are regional specialties in aguas frescas based on what the land has to offer. Veracruz has *agua de jobo*, made with a fruit similar to plums; Yucatán has *agua de piña con chaya*, made with pineapple and *chaya* leaves, which are a bit like spinach; Oaxaca has *agua de chilacayote*, made with a type of squash; and Colima has *horchata de coconut*, a coconut cooler, as well as *bate*, made from toasted, hand-ground chan seeds (similar to chia seeds) and *piloncillo* (a Mexican brown sugar). However, the most popular flavors, tamarind, hibiscus, and *horchata de arroz* (a rice drink with cinnamon), are usually available everywhere. And when my cousin Jorge started a bottled agua fresca company several years ago, called Cañita, his first two flavors were hibiscus and tamarind. His aguas frescas are all natural and truly delicious, with no peeling or soaking required.

Here are a few things to keep in mind when making aguas frescas: Try to use fruits that are in season (though this may not be possible with tropical fruits). The riper the fruit, the tastier your beverage will be and the less sugar you'll need. Use the recipe as a baseline, but adjust the sweetness according to your taste and the ripeness of the fruit, keeping in mind that these beverages aren't meant to be desserts, so they shouldn't be overly sweet. These drinks are generally served over ice, but if you make a large batch, keep in mind that the ice will dissolve and dilute some of the flavor. There are a few ways around this. One is to freeze part of the drink into ice cubes. Another is to refrigerate the beverage until completely chilled before serving so you need less ice—and so the ice you add doesn't melt as quickly. Or you can simply use a bit less water when you make the recipe.

PALETAS
ICE POPS

paletas de fresa
strawberry ice pops

MAKES 8 TO 10

This is probably one of the most common paletas—maybe because the flavor is so kid- and adult-friendly. Strawberry paletas have been my brother's favorite since he was a kid.

The best strawberries in Mexico are from Irapuato; they're a kind of wild strawberry that sweetens the air, and people travel from all over to get big baskets of them. If you are lucky enough to have access to wild strawberries, which are smaller than those that you find at grocery stores but have intensely concentrated sweet flavor, please use them to make these paletas. They are so good and also quite delicate, so they squish easily—perfect for our purposes.

---

4 cups fresh strawberries, preferably wild,
    hulled and cut into quarters
3/4 cup sugar
1/2 cup water
2 tablespoons freshly squeezed lemon juice

Combine the strawberries and sugar in a bowl. Let sit until the strawberries start releasing their natural juices, 20 to 30 minutes. Place in a saucepan with the water over medium heat. Simmer until they are slightly softened, about 5 minutes. Let cool to room temperature.

Transfer the mixture to a blender or food processor, add the lemon juice, and puree until smooth; alternatively, you could leave some chunks in if you like.

If using conventional molds, divide the mixture among the molds, snap on the lid, and freeze until solid, about 5 hours. If using glasses or other unconventional molds, freeze until the pops are beginning to set (1½ to 2 hours), then insert the sticks and freeze until solid, 4 to 5 hours. If using an instant ice pop maker, follow the manufacturer's instructions.

paletas de zarzamora
blackberry ice pops

MAKES 8 TO 10

A few hours outside of Mexico City lies the lakeside town of Valle de Bravo. Many people escape there for the weekend to get some fresh air and enjoy the lake and the chilly mornings in the mountains. We had some family friends who had a country house there. What I looked forward to most when we visited were the incredible wild blackberries, bursting with juice and with a slight tartness that I loved. I always had blackberry smoothies for breakfast and as many of these paletas as I could get. In this recipe, the mixture isn't strained. Part of the awesomeness is enjoying the little seeds in every bite.

4 cups blackberries, fresh or frozen
1^2/$_3$ cups water
^{2}/$_3$ cup sugar
Pinch of salt
2 teaspoons freshly squeezed lemon juice

Put the blackberries, water, sugar, and salt in a blender and blend until smooth. Stir in the lemon juice.

If using conventional molds, divide the mixture among the molds, snap on the lid, and freeze until solid, about 5 hours. If using glasses or other unconventional molds, freeze until the pops are beginning to set (1½ to 2 hours), then insert the sticks and freeze until solid, 4 to 5 hours. If using an instant ice pop maker, follow the manufacturer's instructions.

paletas de melón
cantaloupe ice pops

I love that time near the end of summer when a walk through the market is filled with the smell of sweet juices, drawing you toward the big mountains of melons! For the sweetest paletas, pick melons that smell quite fragrant when you hold them close to you.

$1/2$ cup water
$1/2$ cup sugar
4 cups chopped fresh cantaloupe (about 1 small cantaloupe)
1 tablespoon freshly squeezed lemon juice
Pinch of salt

Combine the water and sugar in a small saucepan. Cook over medium-high heat, stirring, until the mixture comes to a boil and the sugar has dissolved. Let cool to room temperature.

Pour the syrup into a food processor or blender. Add the melon, lemon juice, and salt and blend until smooth.

If using conventional molds, divide the mixture among the molds, snap on the lid, and freeze until solid, about 5 hours. If using glasses or other unconventional molds, freeze until the pops are beginning to set (1½ to 2 hours), then insert the sticks and freeze until solid, 4 to 5 hours. If using an instant ice pop maker, follow the manufacturer's instructions.

paletas de sandía
watermelon ice pops

MAKES 8 TO 10

These incredibly refreshing paletas are quite easy to make. In Mexico, they typically include the watermelon seeds, which are blended along with the flesh, but feel free to use a seedless melon or remove the seeds if you prefer.

$^1/_2$ cup water
$^1/_2$ cup sugar
1$^1/_2$ pounds peeled and diced watermelon (about 4 cups)
1 tablespoon freshly squeezed lime juice
Pinch of salt

Combine the water and sugar in a small saucepan and cook over medium-high heat, stirring, until the mixture comes to a boil and the sugar has dissolved. Let cool to room temperature.

Pour the syrup into a blender. Add the watermelon, lime juice, and salt and blend until smooth.

If using conventional molds, divide the mixture among the molds, snap on the lid, and freeze until solid, about 5 hours. If using glasses or other unconventional molds, freeze until the pops are beginning to set (1½ to 2 hours), then insert the sticks and freeze until solid, 4 to 5 hours. If using an instant ice pop maker, follow the manufacturer's instructions.

paletas de toronja
grapefruit ice pops

MAKES 8 TO 10

My childhood friend, Dan, loves grapefruit paletas and he kept ask-
ing me when La Newyorkina would have them available at the market.
They did make a short appearance there, but I also promised I would
include this recipe in the book. These slightly bitter ice pops are incredibly refreshing. I prefer to use Ruby Red grapefruit juice because it tends
to be a bit sweeter and has a prettier color.

3/4 cup water

1 cup sugar

2 cups freshly squeezed grapefruit juice, preferably Ruby Red
(about 4 grapefruits)

Combine the water and sugar in a small saucepan. Cook over
medium heat, stirring, until it comes to a boil and the sugar
has dissolved. Let cool to room temperature. Stir in the grapefruit juice.

If using conventional molds, divide the mixture among the
molds, snap on the lid, and freeze until solid, about 5 hours. If
using glasses or other unconventional molds, freeze until the
pops are beginning to set (1½ to 2 hours), then insert the sticks
and freeze until solid, 4 to 5 hours. If using an instant ice pop
maker, follow the manufacturer's instructions.

paletas de aguacate
avocado ice pops

MAKES 8 TO 10

Avocado ice cream is fairly common in Mexico, so I decided to make avocado one of the flavors of paletas when I launched my company La Newyorkina ("the girl from New York") at the Hester Street Fair in New York City's Lower East Side. I was unsure of how people would receive them, but avocado paletas rapidly became a customer and personal favorite!

An avocado ice pop may sound unusual, but it's very tasty and has a luscious creamy texture without any dairy. The lime juice not only helps keep the paleta green, it also enhances the flavor of the avocados.

---

1 cup water
1/2 cup sugar
2 small ripe avocados
Pinch of salt
2 tablespoons freshly squeezed lime juice

Combine the water and sugar in a small saucepan and cook over medium-high heat, stirring, until the mixture comes to a boil and the sugar has dissolved. Let cool to room temperature.

Cut the avocados in half lengthwise. Remove the pit and scoop the flesh into a blender, along with the cooled syrup and salt. Blend until smooth, scraping the sides as needed. Add the lime juice and blend just until combined.

If using conventional molds, divide the mixture among the molds, snap on the lid, and freeze until solid, about 5 hours. If using glasses or other unconventional molds, freeze until the pops are beginning to set (1½ to 2 hours), then insert the sticks and freeze until solid, 4 to 5 hours. If using an instant ice pop maker, follow the manufacturer's instructions.

paletas de limón
lime ice pops

MAKES 8 TO 10

Mexicans can never have enough limes. We put them in everything, so it's no surprise that this flavor of paleta is one of the top three sellers everywhere. For this recipe, try to use the smaller limes, similar to Key limes, as they're a little more tart. That said, these ice pops will be delicious with any lime juice as long as it's freshly squeezed.

---

2 cups water

2/3 cup sugar

3 (1-inch) strips of lime zest

3/4 cup freshly squeezed lime juice (about 10 small limes)

Combine the water, sugar, and lime zest in a small nonreactive saucepan. Cook, stirring, over medium heat until the mixture comes to a boil and the sugar has dissolved. Let cool to room temperature. Strain through a fine-mesh sieve, then stir in the lime juice.

If using conventional molds, divide the mixture among the molds, snap on the lid, and freeze until solid, about 5 hours. If using glasses or other unconventional molds, freeze until the pops are beginning to set (1½ to 2 hours), then insert the sticks and freeze until solid, 4 to 5 hours. If using an instant ice pop maker, follow the manufacturer's instructions.

paletas de chabacano y manzanilla
apricot-chamomile ice pops

MAKES 8 TO 10

I can't remember where I first tasted apricots and chamomile together, only that it was in a tart. I loved the combination so much that I decided to make a paleta inspired by it. The natural sweetness of the apricots is enhanced by cooking, and their slight acidity complements the subtle, fragrant flavor of the chamomile. Perhaps it's a combination that is meant to be, since they're in season at farmers' markets at the same time.

---

1 1/2 cups water
1/2 cup sugar
1/3 cup fresh chamomile flowers (1/2 cup dried)
1 pound apricots, pitted and quartered (10 to 12 apricots)
1 tablespoon freshly squeezed lemon juice

Combine the water and sugar in a saucepan and cook over medium heat, stirring, until the mixture comes to a boil and the sugar has dissolved. Stir in the chamomile, lower the heat, and simmer for 10 minutes.

Strain through a fine-mesh sieve, pressing with the back of a wooden spoon to extract as much liquid as possible, then return the syrup to the pot. Stir in the apricots and cook over medium heat, stirring occasionally, until the apricots soften, 5 to 10 minutes. Let cool until lukewarm. Stir in the lemon juice.

Pour the mixture into a blender or food processor and blend until it's smooth (it's fine to leave it chunky, if you prefer). Refrigerate until completely chilled.

If using conventional molds, divide the mixture among the molds, snap on the lid, and freeze until solid, about 5 hours. If using glasses or other unconventional molds, freeze until the pops are beginning to set (1½ to 2 hours), then insert the sticks and freeze until solid, 4 to 5 hours. If using an instant ice pop maker, follow the manufacturer's instructions.

paletas de jamaica con frambuesa
hibiscus-raspberry ice pops

MAKES 8 TO 10

Hibiscus is a flavor that you could say is quintessentially Mexican. Hibiscus paletas are widely available, but not with raspberries. My friend Hannah thought these two flavors would be awesome together, and she was right. (Thanks, Hannah!) We spent a lot of time figuring out different ways to blend the two flavors: cooking the berries in a bit of the agua de jamaica, macerating or mashing them together, and using frozen versus fresh berries. I kept experimenting and found that mixing the raspberries with the sugar and letting them sit for a while helped draw out their juices. Then, when you pour in the agua de jamaica, the juices blend, so you get both flavors in every bite.

---

2 cups agua de jamaica (page 97)
$2/3$ cup sugar
4 cups raspberries, fresh or frozen

Combine the agua de jamaica and $\frac{1}{3}$ cup of the sugar in a small saucepan. Cook over medium heat, stirring, just until the sugar dissolves. Let cool slightly, then refrigerate until chilled.

Mix the raspberries with the remaining $\frac{1}{3}$ cup sugar and let sit until the berries release some of their juices, about 30 minutes.

Divide the raspberries and their juices evenly among the molds, then pour in the agua de jamaica mixture, dividing it evenly among the molds. If using conventional molds, snap on the lid and freeze until solid, about 5 hours. If using glasses or other unconventional molds, freeze until the pops are beginning to set ($1\frac{1}{2}$ to 2 hours), then insert the sticks and freeze until solid, 4 to 5 hours. If using an instant ice pop maker, follow the manufacturer's instructions.

paletas de piña con chile
spicy pineapple ice pops

MAKES 8 TO 10

In Mexico, fruit and chiles are often found together: in fruit stands, where ground chiles are sprinkled over freshly cut fruit; in fruit-flavored lollipops covered with ground chiles; and in many different ice pops. The spiciness in these ice pops comes from a chile-infused syrup and chunks of fresh pineapple tossed with ground chiles, so they have different layers of flavor and spiciness.

---

1 cup water
$1/2$ cup sugar
1 small serrano or jalapeño pepper, split lengthwise
1 ripe pineapple, peeled
2 tablespoons freshly squeezed lime juice
1 to 2 teaspoons ground chiles (piquín, guajillo, or árbol)
$1/2$ teaspoon salt

Combine the water and sugar in a small saucepan. Cook over medium-high heat, stirring, until the mixture comes to a boil and the sugar has dissolved. Add the serrano, lower the heat, and simmer for 5 minutes. Let cool to room temperature. Strain through a fine-mesh sieve.

Finely dice 1½ cups of the pineapple and coarsely chop the rest. Mixed the diced pineapple with the chile and salt and set aside. Put the coarsely chopped pineapple in a blender or food processor, pour in the syrup, lime juice, and blend until smooth.

Divide the blended mixture among the molds, leaving enough room for the diced pineapple. If using conventional molds, don't snap on the lids yet. Freeze until the mixture has a slushy consistency, about 30 minutes. (This will prevent the diced pineapple from sinking to the bottom when added.)

(continued)

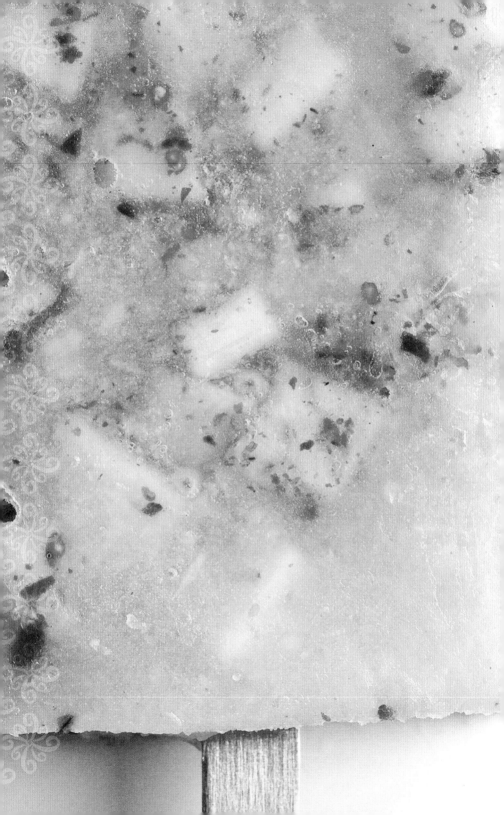

Drop the diced pineapple into the ice pops, dividing it evenly among the molds. If it floats, push it down with a small spoon or an ice pop stick.

If using conventional molds, snap on the lid and freeze until solid, about 5 hours. If using glasses or other unconventional molds, freeze until the pops are beginning to set (45 minutes to 1 hour), then insert the sticks and freeze until solid, 3 to 4 hours. If using an instant ice pop maker, mix the diced pineapple in with the blended mixture, then pour into the molds and follow the manufacturer's instructions.

paletas de donají
mezcal-orange ice pops

MAKES 8 TO 10

Donají is a delicious traditional beverage in the state of Oaxaca, named after a Zapotec princess. The exact ingredients of this cocktail vary, but typically it contains mezcal and orange juice and is served in a glass rimmed with *sal de gusano*, a powdered combination of chiles, salt, and roasted *gusano*, a caterpillar that lives on the agave plant. It may sound strange, but it is so good. If you ever travel to Oaxaca, you must try it. Although I haven't seen *donají* offered as a paleta flavor anywhere, I think it's only a matter of time, because the combination is delicious.

3/4 cup water
3/4 cup sugar
1 1/4 cups freshly squeezed orange juice (about 5 oranges)
2 tablespoons freshly squeezed lime juice
1/3 cup mezcal
1 tablespoon kosher salt
1/4 teaspoon ground chile (piquín or árbol)

Combine the water and sugar in a small saucepan. Cook over medium-high heat, stirring, until the mixture comes to a boil and the sugar has dissolved. Let cool to room temperature. Stir in the orange juice, lime juice, and mezcal.

If using conventional molds, divide the mixture among the molds, snap on the lid, and freeze until solid, about 5 hours. If using glasses or other unconventional molds, freeze until the pops are beginning to set (1½ to 2 hours), then insert the sticks and freeze until solid, 4 to 5 hours. If using an instant ice pop maker, follow the manufacturer's instructions.

To serve the paletas, mix together the salt and chile powder and either sprinkle it over the paletas or dip the tips into the mixture.

paletas de sangrita
spiced tomato-tequila ice pops

MAKES 10 TO 12

Sangrita, a spiced tomato drink served as a chaser for tequila, inspired this delicious paleta. For the sweetest and tastiest ice pops, make this recipe when tomatoes are at the peak of their season. To make the tomato puree, just remove the stems from perfectly ripe tomatoes, trim the tomatoes if needed, rinse them, then process in a blender or food processor.

---

1 cup water
$^2/_3$ cup sugar
2 cups pureed ripe tomatoes (about 5 tomatoes)
$^1/_3$ cup silver or blanco tequila
$^1/_4$ cup freshly squeezed lime juice (about 3 limes)
3 tablespoons hot sauce (choose a brand that isn't too vinegary, such as Cholula, Tapatío, or Valentina)
$^1/_2$ teaspoon salt

Combine the water and sugar in a small saucepan. Cook over medium-high heat, stirring, until the mixture comes to a boil and the sugar has dissolved. Let cool to room temperature.

Combine the tomatoes, tequila, lime juice, hot sauce, salt, and syrup in a large bowl and stir until well combined.

If using conventional molds, divide the mixture among the molds, snap on the lid, and freeze until solid, about 5 hours. If using glasses or other unconventional molds, freeze until the pops are beginning to set (1½ to 2 hours), then insert the sticks and freeze until solid, 4 to 5 hours. If using an instant ice pop maker, follow the manufacturer's instructions.

paletas de crema y cereza con tequila
sour cream, cherry, and tequila ice pops

MAKES 8 TO 10

This definitely isn't a common flavor of paletas in Mexico! It's inspired by one of the first desserts that wowed me as a child—and my favorite dessert for years: cherries jubilee. My extended family and I were on a cruise, and one night all the waiters came out to make cherries jubilee, flambéing the cherries tableside, then serving them over vanilla ice cream. It was quite a theatrical spectacle to see all the elegant waiters simultaneously come out of nowhere with their carts. I was more impressed by the amazing flavors than the dramatic flair. Back then, I was too young to know the word *sublime*, but that's definitely how I felt when I ate it. In this version, sour cream replaces the vanilla ice cream. Its tart flavor complements the sweet cherries deliciously.

8 ounces stemmed and pitted cherries, fresh or frozen

1/3 cup confectioners' sugar

2 teaspoons freshly squeezed lemon juice

2 tablespoons silver or blanco tequila

1 1/2 cups whole milk

1/2 cup granulated sugar

1/4 teaspoon salt

1 vanilla bean, split lengthwise, or 1 teaspoon pure vanilla extract

1 1/2 cups sour cream

Put the cherries in a nonreactive saucepan with the confectioners' sugar and cook over medium heat, stirring, until the mixture comes to a boil and the sugar has dissolved. Lower the heat, stir in the lemon juice, and simmer, stirring often, until the syrup has thickened and has a consistency like maple syrup. Remove from the heat, stir in the tequila, and refrigerate until completely chilled. *(continued)*

Drain the cherries, reserving the liquid for another use (like a yummy raspado!). Combine the milk, granulated sugar, and salt in a medium saucepan. If using the vanilla bean, scrape the seeds into the mixture, then add the pod. Cook over medium heat, stirring, until the sugar has dissolved and the mixture just comes to a boil.

Remove from the heat, add the sour cream, and stir with a whisk until completely smooth. If using vanilla extract, stir it in at this point. Let cool slightly, then discard the vanilla bean pod and refrigerate the mixture until completely chilled.

Put a bit of the sour cream mixture into each of the molds, to a height of about 1 inch. Freeze until the mixture begins to set, about 30 minutes.

Divide the drained cherries among the molds, then pour in the remaining sour cream mixture, dividing it evenly among the molds.

If using conventional molds, snap on the lid and freeze until solid, 3 to 4 hours. If using glasses or other unconventional molds, freeze until the pops are beginning to set (45 minutes to 1 hour), then insert the sticks and freeze until solid, 3 to 4 hours. If using an instant ice pop maker, mix the cherries with the sour cream mixture before pouring it into the molds, then follow the manufacturer's instructions.

paletas de yogurt con moras
yogurt ice pops with berries

MAKES 8 TO 10

The Greek-style yogurt provides a creamy consistency for this paleta, so you'll have a rich mouthfeel without any of the guilt. This combination is really quite classic, but feel free to replace the blackberries with any other berry.

If you want a marbled paleta, put the blackberries in a blender and sprinkle with confectioners' sugar to taste (just a little sweet) and whirl. Pour the mixture into the molds after adding the yogurt mixture, swirling with a skewer while you pour (see page 42).

---

1 lemon
1/2 cup water
1/2 cup sugar
1 1/2 cups plain unsweetened Greek-style yogurt
2 tablespoons honey
2 cups fresh blackberries, or the berry of your choice

Rinse the lemon, then peel it. (This recipe uses only the peel, so save the lemon for a different use.) Combine the water and sugar in a small saucepan. Cook over medium-high heat, stirring, until the mixture comes to a boil and the sugar has dissolved. Add the lemon peel, lower the heat, and simmer for 5 minutes. Let cool to room temperature. Strain the syrup through a fine-mesh sieve, then refrigerate until chilled.

Put the yogurt and honey in a blender, add the chilled syrup, and blend to combine. Pour a bit of the yogurt mixture into each of the molds, to a height of about ¾ inch. Freeze until the mixture begins to set, about 40 minutes.

If the blackberries are big, cut them in half. Divide the blackberries among the molds, then pour in the remaining yogurt mixture, dividing it evenly among the molds. *(continued)*

If using conventional molds, snap on the lid and freeze until solid, 3 to 4 hours. If using glasses or other unconventional molds, freeze until the pops are beginning to set (45 minutes to 1 hour), then insert the sticks and freeze until solid, 3 to 4 hours.

If using an instant ice pop maker, gently fold the blackberries into the yogurt prior to filling the molds and follow the manufacturer's instructions.

 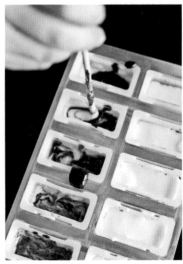

paletas de plátano rostizado
roasted banana ice pops

MAKES 8 TO 10

You're probably familiar with the little tune that announces the ice cream truck is coming down the street. In Mexico, there's a specific whistle (admittedly, not at all pleasant) that lets you know a cart with warm sweet potatoes and plantains is on its way. The purveyors wander through the streets pushing carts that steam the sweet potatoes and plantains in their skins. The whistle is the cry of the steam coming out. For this recipe, you can use either bananas or plantains. Either way, roasting heightens their sweetness and gives them a more complex flavor. If you use plantains, be sure to buy ripe ones: they look black on the outside and feel mushy.

---

3 ripe bananas, or 2 small ripe plantains
1/4 cup packed dark brown sugar
2 tablespoons granulated sugar
1 cup whole milk
1/2 cup heavy cream
3/4 teaspoon pure vanilla extract
1 teaspoon freshly squeezed lemon juice
1 teaspoon Mexican cinnamon
Pinch of salt
1 tablespoon dark rum (optional)

Preheat the oven to 400°F. Wrap the bananas (with their skins still on) in foil individually. Roast until cooked through and soft (use tongs to test), about 30 minutes for bananas and 40 minutes for plantains.

Let sit just until cool enough to handle. Put the flesh in a bowl, discard the peels, and mash the flesh lightly with a fork. Add the brown sugar and granulated sugar and stir until the sugars have dissolved. *(continued)*

Put the banana mixture in a blender. Add the milk, cream, vanilla, lemon juice, cinnamon, salt, and rum and blend until smooth. Let cool slightly, then refrigerate until completely chilled.

If using conventional molds, divide the mixture among the molds, snap on the lid, and freeze until solid, about 5 hours. If using glasses or other unconventional molds, freeze until the pops are beginning to set (1½ to 2 hours), then insert the sticks and freeze until solid, 4 to 5 hours. If using an instant ice pop maker, follow the manufacturer's instructions.

paletas de maracuyá
passion fruit cream pops

MAKES 8 TO 10

Passion fruit really lives up to its name, and its incomparable flavor becomes even more sublime in this paleta, where its tartness cuts through the richness of the creamy base. If you're lucky enough to find fresh ripe passion fruit, buy it, because you can always store the puree in the freezer. To use passion fruit, simply cut it in half and scoop out the flesh. Otherwise, look for frozen passion fruit pulp in ethnic or specialty markets, as well as online, making sure that what you buy is just pulp, with no sugar added. If you want a little crunch and texture, use the passion fruit seeds.

$^2/_3$ cup passion fruit pulp, frozen or from fresh fruits
    (8 to 10 fresh fruits)
1$^1/_2$ cups half-and-half
$^2/_3$ cup sugar
Pinch of salt
1 vanilla bean, split lengthwise, or $^3/_4$ teaspoon pure vanilla extract
3 egg yolks
$^1/_4$ cup passion fruit seeds (optional)

Put the passion fruit pulp and ½ cup of the half-and-half in a bowl and stir to combine.

Combine the remaining 1 cup half-and-half and the sugar and salt in a small saucepan. If using a vanilla bean, scrape the seeds into the mixture, then add the pod. Cook over medium heat, stirring, until the sugar has dissolved and the mixture just comes to a boil. *(continued)*

Meanwhile, whisk the egg yolks in a bowl large enough to accommodate the half-and-half mixture. When the half-and-half mixture begins to boil, slowly pour the warm liquid into the yolks while whisking continuously to avoid making scrambled eggs! Pour the mixture back into the pot and cook over medium-low heat, stirring continuously, until the mixture thickens and coats the back of a spoon. If using vanilla extract, stir it in at this point.

Strain through a fine-mesh sieve. Add the passion fruit mixture and whisk lightly until thoroughly combined. Let cool over an ice bath, stirring occasionally, then refrigerate until completely chilled. Stir in the passion fruit seeds.

If using conventional molds, divide the mixture among the molds, snap on the lid, and freeze until solid, about 5 hours. If using glasses or other unconventional molds, freeze until the pops are beginning to set (1½ to 2 hours), then insert the sticks and freeze until solid, 4 to 5 hours. If using an instant ice pop maker, follow the manufacturer's instructions.

paletas de pay de limón
lime pie ice pops

MAKES 8 TO 10

These paletas are quick to make. The only effort is in squeezing the limes, and it's worth it. Don't use that bottled stuff or the flavor will suffer. Lime pie isn't a typical paleta flavor, but the pie itself is popular. I wanted to make it into a paleta, and the result is this creamy, lip-smacking treat.

---

1 (14-ounce) can sweetened condensed milk
1 cup half-and-half
3/4 cup freshly squeezed lime juice (about 4 large limes)
2 teaspoons lime zest
Pinch of salt
3 cups coarsely crushed Maria cookies, or graham crackers

Put the sweetened condensed milk, half-and-half, lime juice, lime zest, and salt in a bowl and whisk until thoroughly combined.

If using conventional molds, divide the mixture among the molds, snap on the lid, and freeze until solid, about 5 hours. If using glasses or other unconventional molds, freeze until the pops are beginning to set (1½ to 2 hours), then insert the sticks and freeze until solid, 4 to 5 hours. If using an instant ice pop maker, follow the manufacturer's instructions.

Spread the graham cracker pieces on a large plate. Unmold the paletas and press each side into the graham crackers, coating completely.

paletas de coco rápidas
quick coconut ice pops

MAKES 6 TO 8

Coconut is one of the most popular paleta flavors, so I decided to
include two coconut ice pop recipes in this book. This quick version is
very creamy and sure to be a crowd-pleaser. It's inspired by a coconut
paleta I had when I last visited the wonderful state of Campeche. It was
a very hot day and I desperately needed to cool off, so I had a coconut
paleta. It was an unusual choice for me, but I was convinced because
the man selling it said that it had toasted shredded coconut mixed in;
I thought the nutty flavor and lovely crunchiness of the toasted coconut
went wonderfully with the rich, smooth coconut base.

---

1 (13.5-ounce) can coconut milk
1 (14-ounce) can sweetened condensed milk
$2/3$ cup half-and-half
$1/4$ teaspoon salt
$1/4$ teaspoon pure vanilla extract
$3/4$ cup unsweetened shredded coconut, lightly toasted (see opposite)

Put the coconut milk, sweetened condensed milk, half-and-
half, salt, and vanilla in a blender and blend until smooth. Stir
in the coconut.

If using conventional molds, divide the mixture among the
molds, snap on the lid, and freeze until solid, about 5 hours. If
using glasses or other unconventional molds, freeze until the
pops are beginning to set (1½ to 2 hours), then insert the sticks
and freeze until solid, 4 to 5 hours. If using an instant ice pop
maker, follow the manufacturer's instructions.

TOASTING COCONUT helps bring out the natural oil, the same way that toasting nuts makes the overall flavor deeper and more complex.

Although you can toast shredded coconut on the stovetop, it tends to burn rapidly. I find that the best approach is to spread a thin layer in a shallow pan or sheet pan and toast in a 325°F oven for 10 to 15 minutes. Move the coconut around every few minutes so that it toasts evenly. You'll know it's done when it gives off a lovely nutty aroma and is golden all over.

If you want to make a sweetened version, toss the shredded coconut with a couple tablespoons of confectioners' sugar before you toast it.

paletas de coco fresco
fresh coconut ice pops

MAKES 10 TO 12

These paletas may seem very time-consuming, but the sweet and subtle flavor of fresh coconut is well worth the effort. You can prepare the shredded coconut up to a week in advance and refrigerate it in an airtight container. Choose a coconut that feels heavy for its size and inspect the eyes, making sure there's no liquid around them, as that indicates a rotten coconut. I usually like to buy two just in case one is bad. The worst thing that can happen is that you have extra coconut, which you can store in the freezer or dry in a 250°F oven to make dried shredded coconut.

---

1 coconut
Pinch of salt (optional)
2 cups very hot water
3 cups whole milk
3/4 cup sugar, or to taste
1 (1-inch) piece Mexican cinnamon
1/4 cup rum or coconut liqueur (optional)

Preheat the oven to 325°F. Place the coconut on a towel with the eyes facing up. Pierce each eye with a screwdriver or ice pick, then empty out the coconut water. (Strain it and reserve for another use, or enjoy it on its own as a cold beverage.) Get out as much liquid as possible by turning the coconut upside down and shaking it.

Put the coconut on a rimmed baking sheet and bake until it begins to crack, 30 to 40 minutes. Remove from the oven and let sit until cool enough to handle. Put the coconut on a towel and use the bottom (nonsharp) edge of a knife or a hammer to tap it all around and help you crack it open. Remove the outer brown shell with your hands, then use a paring knife to remove the thin brown skin. *(continued)*

Cut the cleaned coconut into pieces and shred it using a hand grater or food processor. If you'd like ribbons of coconut inside the paletas, use a vegetable peeler to cut a few thin strips of the roasted coconut before shredding it. Place the strips in a bowl and toss with the salt. Working in batches, blend the coconut with the hot water until as smooth as possible, then strain through a colander or sieve lined with cheesecloth. Squeeze the cheesecloth to extract as much juice as possible, and discard any leftover coconut.

Put the strained liquid in a large saucepan, then stir in the milk, sugar, and cinnamon, and bring to a simmer over medium heat. Lower the heat and simmer, stirring occasionally, for 15 minutes. Keeping in mind that the sweetness will diminish as the mixture cools off, taste and add more sugar if you like. Let cool to room temperature, then strain through a fine-mesh sieve. Stir in the rum.

If using conventional molds, divide the mixture among the molds, snap on the lid, and freeze until solid, about 5 hours. (If you created ribbons of coconut, add them to the molds before adding the liquid.) If using glasses or other unconventional molds, freeze until the pops are beginning to set (1½ to 2 hours), then insert the sticks and freeze until solid, 4 to 5 hours. If using an instant ice pop maker, follow the manufacturer's instructions.

paletas de nuez
pecan ice pops

MAKES 6 TO 8

I had a recipe for pecan paletas in my first cookbook, *My Sweet Mexico*, but I'm including a different version here because this flavor is one of my favorites. These ice pops are a bit sweeter and creamier than the ones in *My Sweet Mexico* because they're made with sweetened condensed milk and half-and-half. Both versions are really delicious, and I'm still debating which I like best. It's hard to find pecan extract here, but if you come across some, I recommend adding 1 teaspoon along with the vanilla for an even deeper nutty flavor.

3 cups half-and-half
1 (14-ounce) can sweetened condensed milk
2 teaspoons pure vanilla extract
1/4 teaspoon salt
2 cups pecans, coarsely chopped

Put the half-and-half, sweetened condensed milk, vanilla, and salt in a bowl and stir to combine. Add 1¼ cups of the pecans and let the mixture sit for about 30 minutes to extract the flavor from the pecans.

Transfer the mixture to a blender and blend until smooth. Strain through a fine-mesh sieve, pressing the solids with a wooden spoon to extract as much flavor as possible.

Divide the mixture among the molds, leaving enough room for the pecans. If using conventional molds, don't snap on the lids yet. Freeze until the mixture has a slushy consistency, about 30 minutes. (This will prevent the pecans from sinking to the bottom.)

Drop the remaining pecan pieces into the ice pops, dividing them evenly among the molds. If they float, push them down with a small spoon or ice pop stick. *(continued)*

If using conventional molds, snap on the lid and freeze until solid, about 3 to 4 hours. If using glasses or other unconventional molds, freeze until the pops are beginning to set (45 minutes to 1 hour), then insert the sticks and freeze until solid, 3 to 4 hours. If using an instant ice pop maker, gently fold the pecan pieces into the strained liquid prior to filling the molds and follow the manufacturer's instructions.

paletas de chocolate
mexican chocolate ice pops

MAKES 6 TO 8

In Mexico, chocolate is mainly used to prepare hot chocolate, so when you hear people say "Mexican chocolate," or *chocolate de mesa*, they usually mean chocolate made for this purpose. It's grainy because it's basically toasted ground cocoa mixed with sugar, cinnamon, and sometimes vanilla, almonds, or both. I really love the fragrance of Mexican cinnamon, so I like to infuse some in the liquid for this ice pop to add more flavor. I decided to add little bits of chocolate and almonds to these paletas to give another layer of flavor and crunchiness. Who doesn't love that?

1 cup heavy cream
2 cups whole milk
1 (3-inch) piece Mexican cinnamon stick
Pinch of salt
8 ounces *chocolate de mesa*, coarsely chopped
3/4 cup toasted almonds, coarsely chopped (optional)

Put the cream, milk, cinnamon, and salt in a saucepan over medium heat. Bring to a simmer, then lower the heat and simmer for 5 minutes. Add 4 ounces of the chocolate and stir until dissolved. Let cool over an ice bath, stirring occasionally. Strain through a fine-mesh sieve and chill completely.

Mix the remaining 4 ounces of chocolate with the almonds.

Divide the cream mixture among the molds, leaving enough room for the almond mixture. If using conventional molds, don't snap on the lids yet. Freeze until the mixture has a slushy consistency, 30 minutes. (This will keep the almond and chocolate mixture from sinking to the bottom.)

Drop the almond mixture into the ice pops, dividing it evenly among the molds. If the pieces float, push them down with a small spoon or ice pop stick. *(continued)*

If using conventional molds, snap on the lid and freeze until solid, 3 to 4 hours. If using glasses or other unconventional molds, freeze until the pops are beginning to set (45 minutes to 1 hour), then insert the sticks and freeze until solid, 3 to 4 hours.

If using an instant ice pop maker, gently fold the chocolate and almonds into the cream mixture prior to filling the molds and follow the manufacturer's instructions.

paletas de rompope
mexican eggnog ice pops

MAKES 10 TO 12

Rompope is a beverage brought to Mexico by nuns in Spanish colonial times. You can purchase it at some U.S. liquor stores, and more widely in Mexico, but making it is fun and you'll surely enjoy the frozen version.

---

2 cups whole milk
2/3 cup sugar
1 (3-inch) piece Mexican cinnamon stick
Pinch of salt
6 egg yolks
1 cup heavy cream
2 tablespoons brandy or rum
2 teaspoons pure vanilla extract

Combine the milk, sugar, cinnamon, and salt in a saucepan and cook over medium heat, stirring, until the mixture comes to a boil and the sugar has dissolved.

Meanwhile, whisk the egg yolks in a bowl large enough to accommodate the milk mixture. Once the milk mixture begins to boil, slowly pour the warm liquid into the yolks while whisking continuously. Pour the mixture back into the pot and cook over medium-low heat, stirring continuously, until the mixture thickens and coats the back of a spoon.

Strain through a fine-mesh sieve. Add the cream and stir until well incorporated. Stir in the liquor and vanilla. Let cool over an ice bath, stirring occasionally, then refrigerate for a few hours.

If using conventional molds, divide the mixture among the molds, snap on the lid, and freeze until solid, about 5 hours. If using glasses or other unconventional molds, freeze until the pops are beginning to set (1½ to 2 hours), then insert the sticks and freeze until solid, 4 to 5 hours. If using an instant ice pop maker, follow the manufacturer's instructions.

paletas de cajeta
caramel ice pops

MAKES 10 TO 12

There are few things in this world that I adore more than *cajeta*, a sticky, sweet goat's milk caramel. It's one of the most delicious treats. I love the slight acidity from the goat's milk, and when combined with the creamy base in this ice pop, it's simply sublime! You can make your own *cajeta* (the recipe is in *My Sweet Mexico*) or you can buy it at ethnic groceries, at specialty markets, or online.

---

3 cups half-and-half
1/3 cup sugar
Pinch of salt
1 vanilla bean, split lengthwise, or 3/4 teaspoon pure vanilla extract
3/4 cup *cajeta*
1 cup coarsely chopped pecans or walnuts (optional)

Combine 1½ cups of the half-and-half with the sugar and salt in a saucepan. If using the vanilla bean, scrape the seeds into the mixture, then add the pod. Cook over medium heat, stirring, until the sugar has dissolved. Remove from the heat and stir in the *cajeta* and the remaining 1½ cups half-and-half. If using vanilla extract, stir it in at this point. Let cool slightly, then discard the vanilla bean pod and refrigerate the mixture until completely chilled.

Divide the mixture among the molds, leaving enough room for the pecans. If using conventional molds, don't snap on the lids yet. Freeze until the mixture has a slushy consistency, about 30 minutes. (This will prevent the pecans from sinking to the bottom.)

Drop the pecans into the ice pops, dividing them evenly among the molds. If they float, push them down with a small spoon or ice pop stick.

If using conventional molds, snap on the lid and freeze until solid, about 3 to 4 hours. If using glasses or other unconventional molds, freeze until the pops are beginning to set (45 minutes to 1 hour), then insert the sticks and freeze until solid, 3 to 4 hours.

If using an instant ice pop maker, gently fold the pecans into the *cajeta* mixture prior to filling the molds and follow the manufacturer's instructions.

paletas de arroz con leche
rice pudding ice pops

MAKES 8 TO 10

If you love rice pudding, you'll adore these paletas. They have a particularly creamy texture because half of the rice pudding is blended after it's cooked. Mmmm, I'm salivating just thinking about it! I give you the option of using cinnamon or lime zest with the vanilla because both are common combinations. I couldn't decide between the two, so I leave it up to you.

$1/2$ cup short- or medium-grain rice
3 cups whole milk
$2/3$ cup heavy cream
$3/4$ cup sugar
1 (3-inch) piece Mexican cinnamon, or 2 (1-inch) strips lime zest
1 vanilla bean, split lengthwise, or $3/4$ teaspoon pure vanilla extract

---

Combine the rice, milk, cream, half of the sugar, and the cinnamon in a large saucepan. If using the vanilla bean, scrape the seeds into the pot, then add the pod. Cook over medium heat, stirring occasionally, until the mixture comes to a simmer. Lower the heat and simmer, stirring often, for 45 minutes. Add the remaining sugar and continue to cook, stirring often so it doesn't stick to the bottom, until the rice is tender. If using vanilla extract, stir it in at this point.

Discard the vanilla bean pod and cinnamon or zest and let cool slightly. Transfer half of the mixture to a blender or food processor and puree until smooth (don't worry if some bits of rice remain). Pour the puree back into the mixture, stir thoroughly, and refrigerate until completely chilled.

If using conventional molds, divide the mixture among the molds, snap on the lid, and freeze until solid, about 5 hours. If using glasses or other unconventional molds, freeze until the pops are beginning to set (1½ to 2 hours), then insert the sticks and freeze until solid, 4 to 5 hours. If using an instant ice pop maker, follow the manufacturer's instructions.

RASPADOS
SHAVED
ICES

raspado de moras
berry shaved ice

MAKES 6 TO 8

This stunning shaved ice is a guaranteed crowd-pleaser. You can make these ahead of time for a party by assembling the shaved ices, then placing them in the freezer for 30 minutes prior to your guests' arrival. (Just make sure they're not in the freezer for too long or the ice will become too hard—and the glass could crack.)

---

6 cups water

3½ cups sugar

¼ cup corn syrup

1 vanilla bean, split lengthwise, or ¾ teaspoon pure vanilla extract (optional)

2 pounds coarsely chopped fresh berries (strawberries, blueberries, raspberries or blackberries), (about 2 cups berries)

Shaved ice

Combine the water, sugar, and corn syrup in a saucepan. If using the vanilla bean, scrape the seeds into the mixture, then add the pod. Cook over medium heat, stirring, until the mixture begins to boil and the sugar has dissolved.

Remove from the heat and let cool for 10 minutes. If using vanilla extract, stir it in at this point. Discard the vanilla bean, then stir in the berries and let the mixture cool to room temperature. Working in batches, transfer the mixture to a blender and blend until pureed, but do not strain. Let chill completely.

For each serving, mound about 1 cup of shaved ice in a serving glass or cup. Drizzle 6 to 8 tablespoons of the berry syrup over the ice and serve immediately.

raspado rojo
red shaved ice

SERVES 6 TO 8

Rojo means "red," and this syrup gets its name from the vibrant color of fresh pomegranates. Similar ices made with grenadine are found all over Mexico, but grenadine is usually made with artificial flavors and colors. I wanted to include a recipe using fresh pomegranates because it's really tasty. You can clean an extra pomegranate and sprinkle the seeds on top of each serving for a lovely garnish.

6 pomegranates
2 cups sugar
2 cups water
2 tablespoons corn syrup
Shaved or crushed ice

Cut the pomegranates into quarters and remove the seeds. Put the seeds in a saucepan, add the sugar, and muddle to extract the pomegranate flavor and form a puree. Stir in the water and corn syrup. Cook over medium heat, stirring, until the mixture is simmering and the sugar has dissolved. Lower the heat and simmer, stirring occasionally, for 10 minutes. Let cool to room temperature. Strain through a fine-mesh sieve.

For each serving, mound about 1 cup of shaved ice in a serving dish. Drizzle 6 to 8 tablespoons of the pomegranate syrup over the ice and serve immediately.

note: The syrup color will vary depending on the pomegranate's ripeness. For a little extra color and fruitiness, coarsely chop 1 pint strawberries and mix with 1/2 cup sugar. Let sit until the sweet juices are extracted, 30 to 40 minutes. Mix the strawberry juices with the cooled syrup (and use the strawberries for topping, if you like).

raspado de tamarindo
tamarind shaved ice

SERVES 8 TO 10

If you've never tried tamarind before, this shaved ice is a great introduction to the fruit because its delicious tartness is balanced with the
sugar. Plus, it's a very popular flavor that's found all around Mexico. It's
also one of the best flavors to prepare *diablitos* or *chamoyadas*, modern
twists on traditional raspados (see opposite).

---

7 cups water
1 1/4 pounds unpeeled tamarind pods (see page 109)
  or 1 pound tamarind pulp with seeds
2 cups sugar
Shaved ice

Put 6 cups of the water and the tamarind in a saucepan and
bring to a boil. Lower the heat and simmer, stirring occasionally, until the mixture has thickened to a paste; this may take
2 to 3 hours. Let cool and strain through a fine-mesh sieve into
a bowl, pressing the solids with the back of a wooden spoon to
extract as much liquid and tamarind pulp as possible. Let cool
to room temperature.

Meanwhile, combine the remaining cup of water with the
sugar in a small saucepan and cook over medium heat until
the mixture comes to a boil and the sugar has dissolved.
Lower the heat and simmer, stirring occasionally, until the
syrup has thickened and has a consistency like corn syrup.
Let cool to room temperature.

Add the syrup to the tamarind mixture and mix thoroughly
with a whisk or handheld blender. Refrigerate until completely
chilled.

For each serving, mound about 1 cup of shaved ice in a serving dish. Drizzle 6 to 8 tablespoons of the tamarind syrup over
the ice and serve immediately.

DIABLITOS literally means "little devils." These shaved ices are made with fruits like tamarind, mango, or strawberry and topped with fresh lime juice, salt, and ground chiles.

CHAMOYADAS, as the name suggests, are prepared with *chamoy*. Essentially, they're *diablitos* served in a glass, with some of the devilish "toppings" in the glass and more on top.

Adored by young Mexicans, *chamoy* is a red liquid that is salty, tart, and sometimes spicy. It is made from pickled fruit (most commonly plums and apricots) and used as a condiment with fresh fruit, sorbets, and raspados—there are even many paletas nowadays with a *chamoy* filling. It is definitely an acquired taste, but is appreciated throughout Mexico. *Chamoy* is made by brining fruit in salt and/or vinegar, straining it, then adding chili powder. Sometimes a portion of the fruit is blended then combined with the mixture to make a thicker paste, or the amount of liquid is adjusted to achieve a thinner consistency, which is the most common.

raspado de orejones
dried apricot shaved ice

SERVES 6 TO 8

This recipe is inspired by a traditional Arab sweet that I adore, made from dried apricots and pistachios. Many of the sweets in Mexico have Arab influences due to the fact that Arabs occupied Spain for more than seven centuries. The Spanish in turn colonized Mexico, bringing some of those Arabic influences with them.

---

2 cups water
1 1/2 cups sugar
1 vanilla bean, split lengthwise, or 3/4 teaspoon pure vanilla extract
1 cup unsulfured dried apricots
Juice of 1 small lime
Shaved ice
1/2 cup toasted pistachios, coarsely chopped

Combine the water and sugar in a saucepan and cook over medium-high heat, stirring, until the mixture comes to a boil and the sugar has dissolved. If using a vanilla bean, scrape the seeds into the syrup, then add the pod. Bring to a boil over medium heat. Boil for 5 minutes, then let cool completely. If using vanilla extract, stir it in at this point.

Meanwhile, put the apricots in a small saucepan and cover with water. Bring to a boil over medium heat. Let cool for 10 minutes, then drain the apricots.

Discard the vanilla bean pod. Put the syrup, half of the apricots, and the lime juice in a blender and blend until smooth. Refrigerate until completely chilled. Coarsely chop the rest of the apricots.

For each serving, mound about 1 cup of shaved ice in a serving dish. Drizzle 6 to 8 tablespoons of the apricot syrup over the ice, and scatter 1 tablespoon chopped apricots and 1 tablespoon pistachios over the top. Serve immediately.

raspado de piña colada
piña colada shaved ice

SERVES 6 TO 8

Perhaps piña coladas are cliché, but there's a reason why they're still very popular: because pineapple and coconut make a perfect combination. I've never been much of a coconut person myself, but my sister absolutely loves them and would always get a virgin piña colada when we went to the beach. Holding a large green coconut that was bigger than her head, she would position herself on a chair, fixing her hair or hat and imagining she was a glamorous movie star. She would then carefully sip through the straw as slowly as she could, but always managed to finish drinking the coconut water within a few minutes. This recipe is for her.

1 cup water
1 cup sugar
$1/2$ cup unsweetened coconut milk (stir the coconut milk well before
  measuring)
$1/3$ cup light rum
1 pineapple, peeled, cored, and diced (about 4 cups)
Shaved or crushed ice
$3/4$ cup unsweetened shredded coconut, lightly toasted (see page 53)

Combine the water and sugar in a small saucepan and cook over medium-high heat, stirring, until the mixture comes to a boil and the sugar has dissolved. Let cool to room temperature.

Put the syrup, coconut milk, rum, and 3 cups of the pineapple in a blender and blend until smooth. Let chill completely.

For each serving, put about 2 tablepoons of the remaining pineapple in a serving dish or glass. Fill halfway with shaved ice, add 2 tablespoons pineapple, then top with shaved ice. If you have pineapple left over, place it on top. Drizzle 6 to 8 tablespoons of the syrup over the top and garnish with the coconut. Serve immediately.

raspado de horchata con fresas
strawberry-horchata shaved ice

SERVES 4 TO 6

This recipe was first published in the *New York Times* as part of an article on different kinds of shaved ice. The paper's *Diner's Journal* blog asked readers to suggest different flavors, and I had to pick one and come up with a recipe. I chose *horchata*, a milky beverage often made with rice, because I thought it would go perfectly with the luscious, juicy strawberries that filled the market stands at that time. It's worth seeking out Mexican cinnamon, as its flavor makes all the difference in this raspado. If you want a stickier, sweeter syrup, add another can of sweetened condensed milk.

1³/₄ cups blanched almonds
³/₄ cup medium-grain rice
3 cups hot water
1 (3-inch) piece Mexican cinnamon stick
1 (14-ounce) can sweetened condensed milk
1 (14-ounce) can evaporated milk
Pinch of salt
2 cups fresh strawberries
Shaved ice
Ground Mexican cinnamon

Preheat the oven to 350°F. Roast ¾ cup of the almonds until golden, about 8 minutes. Let sit until cool enough to handle, then chop coarsely and set aside.

Combine the rice, water, cinnamon stick, and the remaining cup of almonds in a large container. Once the water is cool, cover and refrigerate for at least 5 hours or overnight.

Working in batches, blend the rice mixture with the sweetened condensed milk, evaporated milk, and salt until as smooth as possible. If it's still a little grainy, strain the syrup through a sieve or colander lined with a double layer of cheesecloth. *(continued)*

Just before serving, rinse and hull the strawberries, then mash them lightly with a fork. For each serving, put about 2 tablespoons of the strawberries in a serving dish. Mound about 1 cup of shaved ice on top of the strawberries, then drizzle 3 to 4 tablespoons of the *horchata* syrup over the ice. Top with the toasted almonds and a dusting of cinnamon and serve immediately.

raspado de rompope
mexican eggnog shaved ice

SERVES 6 TO 8

This ice is delicious on its own, but it also goes well with pretty much any kind of chopped fresh fruit. *Rompope* is similar to eggnog (see page 59), but it has a richer texture and the main spice used is delicious canela.

---

2 cups whole milk
1 (3-inch) piece Mexican cinnamon stick
1 cup sugar
2 cups *rompope* (page 59)
Shaved ice

Combine the milk and cinnamon in a saucepan and bring to a boil. Stir in the sugar, lower the heat, and simmer, stirring constantly until the sugar has dissolved. Continue to simmer until reduced by half. Remove from the heat and stir in the *rompope*. Let chill completely.

For each serving, mound about 1 cup of shaved ice in a serving dish. Drizzle 6 to 8 tablespoons of the *rompope* syrup over the ice and serve immediately.

glorias
veracruz-style shaved ice

SERVES 6

Glorias are a typical dessert in Veracruz. Traditionally, they use a syrup made from grosellas, a small red fruit similar to a red currant. Since it's hard to find grosellas outside of Mexico (but by all means use them if you have access!), I used the syrup from the Raspado Rojo as a successful alternative. However, you can also use red currant marmalade by thinning the marmelade with a bit of water and cooking it over low-medium heat until you obtain a light syrup consistency (you can blend it if it's chunky).

I was quite surprised that I liked this concoction because I'd imagined it was going to be super sweet—but the ice helped balanced everything out.

---

3 ripe bananas
2 tablespoons pure vanilla extract
Shaved ice
2¹/₂ cups condensed milk
2¹/₂ cups raspado rojo syrup (page 68)
Freshly ground Mexican cinnamon, to taste (optional)

Peel the bananas and cut them in half crosswise. Put one half in the bottom of each glass then mash with a fork. Pour 1 teaspoon of the vanilla over each and stir to combine.

Place about 1 cup of shaved ice on top of the banana mixture in each cup, then divide the condensed milk among the glasses, pouring gently. Pour the syrup over top and sprinkle with the cinnamon.

mangonadas
spicy mango ice

SERVES 6 TO 8

This type of ice is very popular, and why wouldn't it be? It has the perfect combination of sweet ripe mangoes, spiciness, a little acidity, and saltiness. This recipe calls for *chamoy*, a sauce or condiment made from pickled fruit, usually apricots or plums. *Chamoy* is a little salty and acidic and it's an acquired taste, but I personally love it and encourage you to try it if you haven't.

2 pounds mangoes, peeled and cut into chunks (3 to 5 mangoes)
1 cup sugar
$1/2$ teaspoon salt
Chamoy
Ground piquín or guajillo chiles to taste, plus more for garnish
$1/3$ cup freshly squeezed lime juice (2 to 3 limes)
Coarse salt

Put the mangoes, sugar, and salt in a food processor and process until completely smooth. Pour the puree into a shallow nonreactive container. Freeze completely, about 5 hours. Scoop the frozen mixture into a blender and blend until crushed.

To serve, put a little *chamoy* in a glass or cup, put a little mango ice on top, and layer with some chiles and *chamoy* as desired. Sprinkle the lime juice on top, then dust with ground chiles and salt as desired. Serve immediately.

note: Another way of making *mangonadas* is to put the mango puree in disposable plastic or paper cups and insert ice pop sticks once the mixture begins to freeze. To serve, peel or cut away the cup and put a little *chamoy* on top, squeeze on some fresh lime juice, and sprinkle with ground chile and salt.

granizado de michelada
beer with chile granita

SERVES 4 TO 6

Micheladas, often called cheladas, are drinks made with beer, fresh lime juice, and sometimes chile. *Micheladas especiales*, or cubanas, use the same foundation but add Worcestershire sauce, hot sauce, and Maggy sauce, a popular seasoning that has a salty, caramelized, deep flavor. This raspado is inspired by these popular beverages.

2 small piquín or árbol chiles
3 cups water
$1/2$ cup sugar
Zest and juice of 3 limes, plus juice for wetting the rim
$1/4$ cup chile powder
$1/2$ teaspoon salt
2 cups cold medium-dark beer

Combine the chiles, water, sugar, and lime zest in a saucepan and cook over medium heat, stirring, until the sugar dissolves. Let cool to room temperature, then stir in the lime juice. Strain through a fine-mesh sieve. Pour the mixture into a shallow nonreactive pan and put it in the freezer.

Once the edges start to freeze (about 1 hour), scrape lightly with a fork, bringing the ice crystals from the edges to the center. Return to the freezer and continue scraping every 30 minutes or so, until the mixture is completely frozen and looks like small ice flakes.

Place the chile powder and salt in a bowl and stir. Wet the rim of a glass with lime juice, then dip it in the chile powder. For each serving, place ½ cup of the granita in the prepared glass. Pour about ¼ cup beer over the granita and serve immediately.

note: It's always best to serve granita as soon as it's ready. But if you leave it in the freezer and it hardens, simply take it out of the freezer, let it soften for 5 to 10 minutes, and then scrape it with a fork again.

granizado de queso con manzanas y piloncillo
queso fresco granita with syrupy apples

SERVES 6 TO 8

Whenever I create a new dessert or want to reinterpret a classic one I am often inspired by other cuisines. During a visit to Italy I had a ricotta cheese granita and, although I have never seen one in Mexico, it inspired this raspado. I've incorporated apples, which are a classic pairing with cheese, to make a raspado that is unusual and unexpected—but certainly very, very tasty.

---

3 cups water
2 tablespoons honey
1 cup *queso fresco*
3 tart, crisp apples, such as Crispin or Granny Smith
2 cups apple or pear cider
8 ounces *piloncillo*, chopped, or 1 cup dark brown sugar plus
    1 tablespoon molasses
1 (3-inch) piece Mexican cinnamon
2 tablespoons butter
Pinch of salt
3/4 cup toasted pecans, coarsely chopped

Combine the water and honey in a saucepan and cook over medium heat, stirring, until the honey is dissolved and the mixture reaches 160°F. Let cool for at least 3 hours or overnight.

Put the honey mixture and *queso fresco* in a food processor and blend until smooth. Pour the mixture into a shallow nonreactive pan and put it in the freezer.

Once the edges start to freeze (about 1 hour), scrape lightly with a fork, bringing the ice crystals from the edges to the center. Return to the freezer and continue scraping every 30 minutes or so, until the mixture is completely frozen and looks like small ice flakes.

Meanwhile, peel the apples and dice finely. Combine the cider, *piloncillo*, and cinnamon in a saucepan and cook over medium heat, stirring, until the mixture comes to a boil and the sugar has dissolved. Lower the heat and simmer until the syrup has thickened and has a consistency like maple syrup. Whisk in the butter and salt. Remove from the heat and stir in the apples. Let chill to room temperature.

For each serving, mound about ½ cup of the cheese granita into a glass or cup. Drizzle about 4 tablespoons of the apple syrup over the granita and top with 1 tablespoon of the pecans. Serve immediately.

AGUAS FRESCAS
REFRESHING DRINKS

agua de pepino con limón
cucumber-lime cooler

MAKES ABOUT 8 CUPS

This quick and refreshing drink is great on its own, but it's also a good base for other beverages. Try stirring in some chopped fresh mint, raspberries, honeydew, or pineapple, or a combination. I'm not sure how it works, but rubbing the end really does help remove bitterness from standard cucumbers; the trick doesn't apply to English or Persian cucumbers.

---

1 large cucumber
6 cups water
1/3 cup freshly squeezed lime juice (2 to 3 limes)
1/3 cup sugar, or more if needed

Rinse the cucumber well. Leave the skin on, cut off about ½ inch from one end, and rub the two flat surfaces against each other (this helps remove any bitterness). Discard the end piece and repeat with the other end.

Slice the cucumber, then put it in a blender. Add the water and blend until completely pureed. Strain through a fine-mesh sieve into a pitcher, then add the lime juice and sugar and stir until the sugar is completely dissolved. Taste and add more sugar if you like.

Refrigerate until completely chilled. Serve over ice.

agua de limón con chía
limeade with chia seeds

MAKES ABOUT 5 CUPS

When I first moved to the States, I often had major cravings for this beverage. In Mexico, chia seeds are sold in most markets and spice shops, but I couldn't find them anywhere in the States, and when I tried to explain what they were, people looked at me like I was crazy. Then, late one night when I was watching TV, I saw this thing called the Chia Pet. I had found my seeds!

Chia seeds look like poppy seeds, but when soaked in liquid for a while, they bloom and develop an awesome gummy texture. This limeade is made using the whole lime, which gives it a slight bitterness, but trust me: it's so good you won't want to make it any other way.

---

3 large limes, quartered
4 cups water
1/2 cup sugar, or more if needed
1/4 cup chia seeds

Put the limes, water, and sugar in a blender and pulse 3 to 4 times, just enough to extract the juice from the limes but not crush the skins (which would make the drink too bitter). Strain through a fine-mesh sieve into a pitcher. Taste and add more sugar if you like.

Whisk in the chia seeds and refrigerate for at least 30 minutes, until completely chilled. Stir before serving, then serve over ice.

naranjada
fizzy orange cooler

MAKES ABOUT 4 CUPS

This is essentially a fresh orange cooler with a little sparkling water, so it's kind of like a natural soda. It isn't as bubbly, but it is quite refreshing and flavorful.

2 cups freshly squeezed orange juice (6 to 8 oranges)
$1/3$ cup sugar, or more if needed
2 cups sparkling mineral water

Combine the orange juice and sugar in a pitcher and stir until the sugar has dissolved. Taste and add more sugar if you like.

Refrigerate until completely chilled. Just before serving, add the sparkling water and serve over ice.

conga
mixed fruit punch

MAKES 4 TO 5 CUPS

This is the kind of drink that made me feel like a grown-up when I was little. It feels like a cocktail, but there's no alcohol (though you could certainly add some vodka or rum). You can make it with precut canned pineapple, but it's so much tastier if you get a fresh, whole pineapple and use that.

1/2 ripe pineapple, peeled, cored, and cut into chunks
2 cups freshly squeezed orange juice (6 to 8 oranges)
2 to 3 tablespoons grenadine syrup

Pass the pineapple through a juicer. Strain the juice through a fine-mesh sieve into a pitcher. You should have about 2 cups. Stir in the orange juice.

Serve the punch over ice, drizzling the grenadine over the top so it comes down the sides.

agua de piña con alfalfa y limón
pineapple-alfalfa-lime cooler

MAKES 4 TO 6 CUPS

When I was growing up, my sister and I often went to the market with my mom. There was a great juice stand where they made all kinds of aguas frescas and smoothies. This was my sister's favorite one. It's incredibly refreshing, and really good for you, too. The type of alfalfa used for these drinks resembles wheatgrass and is grown abundantly in Mexico; you may be able to find alfalfa at nurseries and farmers' markets. Pineapple is commonly mixed with a variety of green herbs. In the Yucatan, for example, it's often blended with *chaya*. If you can't find alfalfa or *chaya*, use a couple tablespoons of fresh mint.

1 ripe pineapple, peeled, cored, and cut into chunks
5 ounces alfalfa
1 1/2 cups water, or more if needed
1/3 cup freshly squeezed lime juice (about 3 limes)
1/2 cup sugar, or more if needed
2 tablespoons honey

Put the pineapple chunks, alfalfa, and water in a blender and blend until as smooth as possible. Add the lime juice, sugar, and honey and stir until the sugar has dissolved. Taste and add more sugar if you like. If the consistency is too thick, add a little more water.

Refrigerate until completely chilled. Serve over ice.

agua de guayaba
guava cooler

MAKES ABOUT 8 CUPS

In Mexico, you know that guava season has started when the fruit's sweet aroma perfumes the air. There are many varieties of guavas, and, thankfully, more and more of them are available in the United States. The skin can be yellowish (often with brown spots) or green, and the flesh may be white, yellowish, or pink. Look for guavas that are very fragrant and feel slightly soft but not mushy. They have many tiny seeds, which are edible, so you can choose to leave them in or strain the drink if you prefer. Personally, I always choose with seeds.

1 pound guavas (8 to 10 guavas)
6 cups water
$1/2$ cup sugar, or more if needed
Juice of 1 lime

Rinse the guavas and use the tip of a knife to remove the bottom part that feels a little hard. Coarsely chop the guavas and put them in a blender. Add the water and sugar and blend until completely smooth. Stir in the lime juice. Strain through a fine-mesh sieve into a pitcher, if desired. Taste and add more sugar if you like.

Refrigerate until completely chilled. Serve over ice.

agua de jamaica
hibiscus cooler

MAKES 4 CUPS

This tasty and refreshing drink is made with dried hibiscus flowers, also known as roselle or Jamaican sorrel. Essentially, it's an herbal iced tea, but perhaps the most beautiful one you've ever had, with a brilliant magenta color extracted from the flowers. I like to soak the flowers overnight, as is traditional in my family, because I feel this extracts more of the subtle, tart, berrylike flavor. Once you're done, instead of discarding the hibiscus flowers, save them to snack on. They'll be a little sweet, and I think they're delicious. Just be sure to keep them refrigerated.

1 cup dried hibiscus flowers
4 cups water
1/3 cup sugar, or more if needed

Rinse the flowers in cold water and drain thoroughly. Put them in a saucepan, cover with the water, and let steep for at least 4 hours or overnight.

Bring the mixture to a boil over medium heat, then lower the heat and simmer for 10 minutes. Stir in the sugar and continue to cook, stirring, until the sugar has dissolved. Let cool to room temperature. Strain through a fine-mesh sieve into a pitcher, pressing the solids with the back of a wooden spoon to extract as much liquid as possible. Add water to bring the volume up to 4 cups If the flavor is too intense, add more water as needed. You can also add a little more sugar if you like.

Refrigerate until completely chilled. Serve as is or over ice.

(continued)

TO MAKE A CONCENTRATE, double the amount of hibiscus, eliminate the sugar, and cook the mixture down until the liquid is reduced to one-third. This will keep for several weeks in the refrigerator. To make a beverage, simply put about 1/4 cup of the concentrate in a glass, add about 1 cup water, and sweeten with sugar to taste. Feel free to adjust these amounts to fit your taste.

lágrimas de la virgen
beet cooler with fruits

MAKES ABOUT 12 CUPS

The literal translation of the name of this drink is "the Virgin's tears," as the red color of the beets resembles tears of blood said to have been shed by the Virgin Mary. This beverage originated in the state of Guanajuato, maybe as long ago as the end of the sixteenth century. I found a few different variations, but this one seemed to be the most common, and it's quite special. Although this beverage is customarily prepared during Lent for the festivities of Friday of Sorrows (the Friday before Good Friday), it's a wonderful drink during fall, when beets and apples abound. This recipe makes a large batch to share at your next gathering.

---

4 red beets
8 cups water
1 cup sugar
1 small apple (Fuji or McIntosh), peeled and diced
1 banana, diced
1 small orange, peeled and diced
4 leaves romaine lettuce, cut into thin strips
Juice of 1 lime

Peel the beets. Cut them into chunks and pass them through a juicer (see page 102).

Combine the water and sugar in a pitcher and stir until the sugar has dissolved. Add the beet juice.

Refrigerate until completely chilled. Add the apple, banana, orange, and lettuce, then stir in the lime juice (which will help prevent the fruit from browning). Serve chilled over ice, if desired.

Alternately, divide the mixed diced fruit among the glasses; place the beet water in a pitcher for guests to pour over.

(continued)

IF YOU DON'T HAVE A JUICER, put the unpeeled beets in a baking pan, cover with foil, and roast at 375°F until fork-tender. Let sit until cool enough to handle, then peel them with your hands (the skins will slip off easily). Blend the roasted beets with some of the water. Proceed with the recipe as written.

horchata de pepita de melón
cantaloupe seed horchata

MAKES ABOUT 9 CUPS

Whenever I use canteloupe to make paletas de melón or agua de melón, I like to save the seeds to make this drink. It's quite tasty, and something about it makes me feel energetic.

8 cups water
1/2 cup sugar
5 ounces dried cantaloupe seeds, about 1 cup (see page 104)
1/2 cup plus 1 1/2 tablespoons blanched almonds
1 tablespoon lime zest

Combine the water with the sugar in a saucepan. Cook over medium-high heat, stirring, until the mixture comes to a boil and the sugar has dissolved. Let cool to room temperature.

Put the cantaloupe seeds and almonds in a food processor or spice grinder and process until completely pulverized, with a flourlike texture. Stir the ground seeds and lime zest into the water.

Refrigerate for at least 4 hours or overnight. Stir, then strain into a pitcher through a sieve or colander lined with cheesecloth. Strain again, this time pressing the solids with the back of a wooden spoon to extract as much liquid as possible. Serve over ice. *(continued)*

**TO MAKE THE DRIED CANTALOUPE
SEEDS,** cut a cantaloupe in half and scoop
out the seeds. Rinse the seeds and drain them
thoroughly, then spread them in a single layer
and leave them out in the sun to dry for a full
day. If you can't dry them outside, put them in
the oven at the lowest temperature possible for
4 to 6 hours. Either way, stir them occasionally
so they'll dry completely and evenly. You can use
the cantaloupe flesh to make an agua fresca.
Just blend it with water and sweeten to taste.

polvillo
cacao-corn drink

MAKES ABOUT 5 CUPS

I first tasted this drink in Tabasco, where they grow some of the best cacao, and fell in love with it. It's traditionally made with freshly ground toasted cacao beans, but in this recipe I call for I cocoa powder because it's more readily available. *Pinole* is a flour made from toasted dried corn kernels. It has a wonderful nuttiness and is often mixed with cinnamon and sugar and stirred into water or milk for a delicious beverage. You can find it at specialty grocery stores and online. In Mexico, many people think the natural sweetness of the corn is enough, but I included sugar in this recipe because I think it's more of an acquired taste. Honey is also quite nice in this beverage, so substitute it for the sugar if you prefer.

8 cups water
$^3/_4$ cup sugar
$^1/_2$ cup unsweetened cocoa powder
$^1/_2$ cup *pinole*
1 teaspoon ground Mexican cinnamon

Combine the water and sugar in a pitcher and stir until the sugar has dissolved. Stir in the cocoa powder, *pinole*, and cinnamon.

Refrigerate until completely chilled. Just before serving, whisk the beverage vigorously so it's frothy, or better yet, if you have a *molinillo*, use it instead of the whisk. Serve over ice.

horchata de arroz
cinnamon-rice drink

MAKES ABOUT 6 CUPS

Horchatas, also called *aguas de horchata*, are a popular type of drink in Mexico most commonly made with rice, but they can also be based on many other ingredients, from almonds to barley or oats to coconut—which are also delicious (see page 108). My favorite has always been the kind made with rice. Not only are *horchatas* based on different ingredients, some are made with water, while others use whole milk, sweetened condensed milk, or evaporated milk, or even a combination of milks, in addition to the water or in place of it. I've had many versions, and I like those with some milk because they have a thicker and creamier mouthfeel, so that's what this recipe calls for. But feel free to make it with water only, adjusting the consistency to suit your taste.

2/3 cup medium- or long-grain white rice
3 cups warm water
1 (2-inch) piece Mexican cinnamon stick
1 cup sugar, or more if needed
2 cups whole milk
Ground Mexican cinnamon

Put the rice in a blender or spice grinder and process until completely pulverized, with a flourlike texture. (Alternatively, you can leave the rice whole if you prefer.) Combine the rice powder, warm water, and cinnamon stick and stir with a whisk until well combined. Cover and refrigerate for at least 5 hours or overnight.

Transfer the mixture to a blender and blend until as smooth as possible. It will feel slightly grainy but should not be gritty. Strain into a pitcher through a sieve or colander lined with a couple layers of cheesecloth, pressing the solids with the back of a wooden spoon to extract as much liquid as possible. Stir in the sugar and milk, then taste and add more sugar if you like.
(continued)

Refrigerate until completely chilled. Serve over ice, topped with a sprinkling of the ground cinnamon.

IN DOWNTOWN OAXACA'S Mercado 20 de Noviembre, there's a stand called Doña Casilda, where they add about 2 tablespoons worth of chunks of cantaloupe and red prickly pear and 1 tablespoon of pecans—or a combination of those—to a tall glass of *horchata*, depending on your preference. The prickly pear makes the *horchata* turn a light shade of pink, and the chunks of fruit and pecans complement the *horchata* wonderfully.

Or, to make a coconut *horchata*, add 1/2 cup of ground blanched almonds to the rice powder mixture before you soak it, and 1 cup of fresh coconut flesh when blending the rice mixture. If the consistency is too thick, add water.

To make a nut *horchata*, add 1 cup of raw nuts (almonds, cashews, or peanuts) to the rice powder mixture before soaking, then proceed as directed.

agua de tamarindo
tamarind cooler

MAKES ABOUT 4 CUPS

Tamarind is one of the most common flavors of agua fresca in Mexico, and it's my absolute favorite. Fresh tamarind pods are available at many specialty markets. Those from Asia are sweeter and more velvety and tend to have more pulp, whereas those from Mexico and the Caribbean are much more tart—which is what I love about them! This beverage has a brownish-orange color, but don't be put off by it.

10 ounces tamarind pods (about 10 large pods)
4 cups water
$^{1}/_{2}$ cup sugar, or more if needed

Peel the tamarind pods by hand and discard the outer shell. It's okay if there are still little bits of shell stuck to the flesh, as the beverage will be strained.

Put the tamarind flesh in a saucepan, seeds and all. Add the water, place over medium heat, and bring to a boil. Lower the heat and simmer, stirring occasionally, until the pulp is very soft, about 45 minutes.

Strain through a fine-mesh sieve into a pitcher, pressing the solids with the back of a wooden spoon to extract as much liquid and tamarind pulp as possible. Add the sugar and stir until it dissolves. Taste and add a little more sugar if you like. Let cool to room temperature, then refrigerate until completely chilled. Serve over ice.

INDEX

A

agua de guayaba, 96
agua de jamaica, 97–99
agua de limón con chía, 91
agua de pepino con limón, 89
*agua de piña con alfalfa y
    limón,* 95
agua de tamarindo, 109
aguas frescas
    Beet Cooler with Fruits,
        101–2
    Cacao-Corn Drink, 105
    Cantaloupe Seed Horchata,
        103–4
    Cinnamon-Rice Drink, 107–8
    Coconut Horchata, 108
    Cucumber-Lime Cooler, 89
    description of, 15
    Fizzy Orange Cooler, 92
    Guava Cooler, 96
    Hibiscus Cooler, 97–99
    history of, 15
    ingredients for, 16–17
    Limeade with Chia Seeds, 91
    making, 17
    Mixed Fruit Punch, 94
    Pineapple-Alfalfa-Lime
        Cooler, 95
    Tamarind Cooler, 109
Alcázar, Ignacio, 5
Alcázar, Luis, 5
Alfalfa-Pineapple-Lime
    Cooler, 95

almonds
    Cantaloupe Seed Horchata,
        103–4
    Coconut Horchata, 108
    Mexican Chocolate Ice Pops,
        57–58
    Strawberry-Horchata Shaved
        Ice, 74–76
Andrade, Agustín, 5
apples
    Beet Cooler with Fruits,
        101–2
    Queso Fresco Granita with
        Syrupy Apples, 84–85
apricots
    Apricot-Chamomile Ice
        Pops, 29
    Dried Apricot Shaved Ice, 72
Avocado Ice Pops, 26

B

bananas
    Beet Cooler with Fruits,
        101–2
    Roasted Banana Ice Pops,
        43–44
    Veracruz-Style Shaved Ice, 79
Beer with Chile Granita, 83
Beet Cooler with Fruits, 101–2
berries. *See also individual
        berries*
    Berry Shaved Ice, 67
    Yogurt Ice Pops with Berries,
        40–42

blackberries
    Berry Shaved Ice, 67
    Blackberry Ice Pops, 22
    Yogurt Ice Pops with Berries,
      40–42
blueberries
    Berry Shaved Ice, 67

C

Cacao-Corn Drink, 105
cajeta
    Caramel Ice Pops, 60–61
cantaloupe
    Cantaloupe Ice Pops, 23
    Cantaloupe Seed Horchata,
      103–4
Caramel Ice Pops, 60–61
Chamomile-Apricot Ice
    Pops, 29
chamoy, 80
chamoyadas, 71
Cherry, Sour Cream, and
    Tequila Ice Pops, 37–39
Chia Seeds, Limeade with, 91
chiles
    Beer with Chile Granita, 83
    Spicy Mango Ice, 80
    Spicy Pineapple Ice Pops,
      32–34
chocolate
    Cacao-Corn Drink, 105
    Mexican Chocolate Ice Pops,
      57–58
Cinnamon-Rice Drink, 107–8
coconut
    Coconut Horchata, 108
    Fresh Coconut Ice Pops,
      53–54
    Piña Colada Shaved Ice, 73
    Quick Coconut Ice Pops, 50
    toasting, 51
conga, 94
Corn-Cacao Drink, 105
Cucumber-Lime Cooler, 89

D

diablitos, 71
Dried Apricot Shaved Ice, 72
drinks. *See aguas frescas*

E

eggs
    Mexican Eggnog Ice
      Pops, 59
    Mexican Eggnog Shaved
      Ice, 77

F

Fizzy Orange Cooler, 92
Fresh Coconut Ice Pops, 53–54

G

glorias, 14, 79
graham crackers
    Lime Pie Ice Pops, 48
granitas
    Beer with Chile Granita, 83
    description of, 12, 14
    making, 12, 14
    Queso Fresco Granita with
      Syrupy Apples, 84–85
    serving, 83
granizado de michelada, 83
granizado de queso con
    manzanas y piloncillo,
      84–85
Grapefruit Ice Pops, 25
Guava Cooler, 96

H

hibiscus
    Hibiscus Cooler, 97–99
    Hibiscus-Raspberry Ice
      Pops, 31
horchata, 74, 107
horchata de arroz, 107–8
horchata de pepita de melón,
    103–4

I

ice pops. *See* paletas

J

Jáuregui, Genarito, 5–6

L

lágrimas de la virgen, 101–2
limes
    Beer with Chile Granita, 83
    Beet Cooler with Fruits,
        101–2
    Cucumber-Lime Cooler, 89
    Limeade with Chia Seeds, 91
    Lime Ice Pops, 28
    Lime Pie Ice Pops, 48
    Pineapple-Alfalfa-Lime
        Cooler, 95
    Spiced Tomato-Tequila Ice
        Pops, 36

M

Malfavón, Rafael, 4
Mango Ice, Spicy, 80
mangonadas, 80
Mexican Chocolate Ice Pops,
    57–58
Mexican Eggnog Ice Pops, 59
Mexican Eggnog Shaved Ice, 77
Mezcal-Orange Ice Pops, 35
Mixed Fruit Punch, 94

N

naranjada, 92

O

oranges
    Fizzy Orange Cooler, 92
    Mezcal-Orange Ice Pops, 35
    Mixed Fruit Punch, 94

P

paletas
    Apricot-Chamomile Ice
        Pops, 29
    Avocado Ice Pops, 26
    Blackberry Ice Pops, 22
    Cantaloupe Ice Pops, 23
    Caramel Ice Pops, 60–61
    description of, 2
    etymology of, 2
    flavors of, 3–4
    freezing, 10
    Fresh Coconut Ice Pops,
        53–54
    Grapefruit Ice Pops, 25
    Hibiscus-Raspberry Ice
        Pops, 31
    history of, 4–6
    ingredients for, 8–9
    Lime Ice Pops, 28
    Lime Pie Ice Pops, 48
    Mexican Chocolate Ice Pops,
        57–58
    Mexican Eggnog Ice Pops, 59
    Mezcal-Orange Ice Pops, 35
    molds for, 9–10
    Passion Fruit Cream Pops,
        45–47
    Pecan Ice Pops, 55–56
    Quick Coconut Ice Pops, 50
    Rice Pudding Ice Pops, 62–63
    Roasted Banana Ice Pops,
        43–44
    Sour Cream, Cherry, and
        Tequila Ice Pops, 37–39
    Spiced Tomato-Tequila Ice
        Pops, 36
    Spicy Pineapple Ice Pops,
        32–34
    Strawberry Ice Pops, 21
    types of, 2
    unmolding, 10–11
    Watermelon Ice Pops, 24

paletas, *continued*
Yogurt Ice Pops with Berries, 40–42
paletas de aguacate, 26
paletas de arroz con leche, 62–63
paletas de cajeta, 60–61
paletas de chabacano y manzanilla, 29
paletas de chocolate, 57–58
paletas de coco fresco, 53–54
paletas de coco rápidas, 50
paletas de crema y cereza con tequila, 37–39
paletas de donají, 35
paletas de fresa, 21
paletas de jamaica con frambuesa, 31
paletas de limón, 28
paletas de maracuyá, 45–47
paletas de melón, 23
paletas de nuez, 55–56
paletas de pay de limón, 48
paletas de piña con chile, 32
paletas de plátano rostizado, 43–44
paletas de rompope, 59
paletas de sandía, 24
paletas de sangrita, 36
paletas de toronja, 25
paletas de yogurt con moras, 40–42
paletas de zarzamora, 22
Passion Fruit Cream Pops, 45–47
pecans
Caramel Ice Pops, 60–61
Pecan Ice Pops, 55–56
Queso Fresco Granita with Syrupy Apples, 84–85
Piña Colada Shaved Ice, 73
pineapple
Mixed Fruit Punch, 94
Piña Colada Shaved Ice, 73
Pineapple-Alfalfa-Lime Cooler, 95

Spicy Pineapple Ice Pops, 32–34
pinole, 105
pistachios
Dried Apricot Shaved Ice, 72
plantains
Roasted Banana Ice Pops, 43–44
polvillo, 105
pomegranates
Red Shaved Ice, 68
Veracruz-Style Shaved Ice, 79

Q
Queso Fresco Granita with Syrupy Apples, 84–85
Quick Coconut Ice Pops, 50

R
raspado de horchata con fresas, 74–76
raspado de moras, 67
raspado de orejones, 72
raspado de piña colada, 73
raspado de rompope, 77
raspado de tamarindo, 70
raspado rojo, 68
raspados
Berry Shaved Ice, 67
description of, 11
Dried Apricot Shaved Ice, 72
etymology of, 11
making, 11–12
Mexican Eggnog Shaved Ice, 77
Piña Colada Shaved Ice, 73
Red Shaved Ice, 68
Spicy Mango Ice, 80
Strawberry-Horchata Shaved Ice, 74–76
syrups for, 12
Tamarind Shaved Ice, 70
Veracruz-Style Shaved Ice, 79

raspberries
  Berry Shaved Ice, 67
  Hibiscus-Raspberry Ice
    Pops, 31
Red Shaved Ice, 68
rice
  Cinnamon-Rice Drink, 107–8
  Coconut Horchata, 108
  Rice Pudding Ice Pops, 62–63
  Strawberry-Horchata Shaved
    Ice, 74–76
Rios, Tilde, 6
Roasted Banana Ice Pops,
  43–44
rompope, 59, 77
rum
  Fresh Coconut Ice Pops,
    53–54
  Mexican Eggnog Ice Pops, 59
  Piña Colada Shaved Ice, 73

S

shaved ice. *See* raspados
Sour Cream, Cherry, and
    Tequila Ice Pops, 37–39
Spiced Tomato-Tequila Ice
    Pops, 36
Spicy Mango Ice, 80
Spicy Pineapple Ice Pops,
    32–34
strawberries
  Berry Shaved Ice, 67
  Strawberry-Horchata Shaved
    Ice, 74–76
  Strawberry Ice Pops, 21

T

tamarind
  Tamarind Cooler, 109
  Tamarind Shaved Ice, 70
tequila
  Sour Cream, Cherry, and
    Tequila Ice Pops, 37–39
  Spiced Tomato-Tequila Ice
    Pops, 36
  Tomato-Tequila Ice Pops,
    Spiced, 36

V

Veracruz-Style Shaved Ice, 79

W

walnuts
  Caramel Ice Pops, 60–61
Watermelon Ice Pops, 24

Y

Yogurt Ice Pops with Berries,
  40–42

MEASUREMENT CONVERSION CHARTS

volume

U.S.	IMPERIAL	METRIC
1 tablespoon	$1/2$ fl oz	15 ml
2 tablespoons	1 fl oz	30 ml
$1/4$ cup	2 fl oz	60 ml
$1/3$ cup	3 fl oz	90 ml
$1/2$ cup	4 fl oz	120 ml
$2/3$ cup	5 fl oz ($1/4$ pint)	150 ml
$3/4$ cup	6 fl oz	180 ml
1 cup	8 fl oz ($1/3$ pint)	240 ml
$11/4$ cups	10 fl oz ($1/2$ pint)	300 ml
2 cups (1 pint)	16 fl oz ($2/3$ pint)	480 ml
$21/2$ cups	20 fl oz (1 pint)	600 ml
1 quart	32 fl oz ($12/3$ pint)	1 l

weight

U.S./IMPERIAL	METRIC
$1/2$ oz	15 g
1 oz	30 g
2 oz	60 g
$1/4$ lb	115 g
$1/3$ lb	150 g
$1/2$ lb	225 g
$3/4$ lb	350 g
1 lb	450 g

length

INCH	METRIC
1/4 inch	6 mm
1/2 inch	1.25 cm
3/4 inch	2 cm
1 inch	2.5 cm
6 inches (1/2 foot)	15 cm
12 inches (1 foot)	30 cm

temperature

FAHRENHEIT	CELSIUS/GAS MARK
250°F	120°C / gas mark 1/2
275°F	135°C / gas mark 1
300°F	150°C / gas mark 2
325°F	160°C / gas mark 3
350°F	180 or 175°C / gas mark 4
375°F	190°C / gas mark 5
400°F	200°C / gas mark 6
425°F	220°C / gas mark 7
450°F	230°C / gas mark 8
475°F	245°C / gas mark 9
500°F	260°C

Para mis queridos hermanos, Yael y Pedro,
por el enorme cariño que existe entre nosotros.

Published in the United States by Ten Speed Press, an imprint of the
Crown Publishing Group, a division of Random House, Inc., New York.
www.crownpublishing.com
www.tenspeed.com

Ten Speed Press and the Ten Speed Press colophon are registered
trademarks of Random House, Inc.

Library of Congress Cataloging-in-Publication Data
Gerson, Fany.
    Paletas : authentic recipes for Mexican ice pops, shaved ice, and
aguas frescas / Fany Gerson ; photography by Ed Anderson and Paul
O'Hanlon. — 1st ed.
        p. cm.
    Includes index.
    Summary: "The first collection of Mexican ice pop (paleta),
shaved ice (raspado), and natural beverage (agua fresca) recipes
for the United States from the country's most authoritative voice on
Mexican sweets, in a user-friendly, engaging package"—Provided by
publisher.
    ISBN 978-1-60774-035-3
    1. Frozen desserts. 2. Ice pops. 3. Beverages. 4. Drinking
water. 5. Cooking, Mexican. I. Title.
    TX795.G47 2011
    641.8'6—dc22

                                                    2010053847

ISBN 978-1-60774-035-3

Printed in China

Design by Katy Brown
Prop styling by Heather Chontos

10 9 8 7 6 5 4 3 2 1

First Edition